SVOBODA: WAGNER

Figure 1. Josef Svoboda in 1979.
Photograph by Jarka Burian.

SVOBODA : WAGNER

Josef Svoboda's Scenography for Richard Wagner's Operas

JARKA BURIAN

WESLEYAN UNIVERSITY PRESS
Middletown, Connecticut

Also by Jarka Burian

THE SCENOGRAPHY OF JOSEF SVOBODA

Copyright © 1983 by Jarka Burian

All uncredited illustrations are used with permission of Josef Svoboda.

All inquiries and permissions requests should be addressed to the Publisher, Wesleyan University Press, 110 Mt. Vernon Street, Middletown, Connecticut 06457

Distributed by Harper & Row Publishers, Keystone Industrial Park, Scranton, Pennsylvania 18512

LIBRARY OF CONGRESS CATALOGING IN PUBLICATION DATA
Burian, Jarka, 1927–
    Svoboda, Wagner: Josef Svoboda's scenography for
Richard Wagner's operas.

    Bibliography: p. 117

    1. Wagner, Richard, 1813–1883. Operas. 2. Svoboda,
Josef, 1925–   . 3. Opera—Production and direction.
I. Title.
ML410.W19B9 1983 782.1'092'4 83-14668
ISBN 0-8195-5088-4

Manufactured in the United States of America
FIRST EDITION

Contents

List of Illustrations

List of Plates

(Between pages 54 and 55)

Preface

This study of Josef Svoboda's scenography for the operas of Richard Wagner is an outgrowth of an acquaintance with Svoboda and his work that dates back to 1965. Since that time I have seen more than sixty of his productions in various parts of Europe and North America. More important, I have had the pleasure of a sustained though intermittent sharing of experiences and ideas with Svoboda: we have exchanged many visits, taught and lectured together, and worked together in the theater. Of prime importance to this study, we have spent countless hours discussing (in his native language) his productions and the thoughts and incidents that accompanied their evolution from initial concepts to final embodiment on stage. I have had full access to his archives and his studio, and frequently I have been able to follow his scenography from initial sketches to models to final rehearsals and opening night, periods interspersed with meetings during which the satisfactions and frustrations of his work became increasingly familiar to me.

The satisfying reception of my initial full-length study, *The Scenography of Josef Svoboda* (1971), prompted the idea of this more specialized sequel, in which Svoboda's creative processes and their technical support might be explored in more detail in relation to a restricted number of productions. In 1972, when a sequel was first considered, Svoboda was about to embark on two separate productions of Wagner's *Ring* cycle, in London and Geneva, and therefore the theme of the sequel—Svoboda's work on Wagner—offered itself with a certain inevitability. By 1972 Svoboda had done four Wagner operas; since then, twelve more. The number is large enough to include a wide range of production challenges and solutions; yet it does not prohibit detailed consideration.

The primary intention of this book is to provide an expanded documentary of the Svoboda-Wagner productions against a background of historical tendencies in the staging of Wagner. Beyond that, however, the intention is to offer certain insights into the ways an unusually gifted, skilled, and productive contemporary scenographer functions. Svoboda has said, "Style is a way of thinking." Underlying specific techniques, materials, and forms are habits of mind and patterns of imagination. Without presuming to understand, much less provide a formula for, Svoboda's special creativity, I believe that I have been close enough to it to gain an awareness and appreciation of many of its aspects, and I hope that I have been able to communicate that awareness and appreciation in this study.

My work on this project received generous assistance

and encouragement from many sources. Barbara Kachur and John Lucas provided substantial assistance in my research into the background of Wagner productions. My colleagues at SUNY Albany, James Leonard and Jerome Hanley, read the first full draft of the manuscript and offered valuable comment. Miroslav Pflug, a former close associate of Svoboda, was very helpful in supplying clarification of certain technical aspects of Svoboda's work. Jaroslav Schneider, Svoboda's secretary, kept me informed of data relating to Svoboda's often complex production schedules and also helped with translation from the German, as did my colleague Peter Benedict.

My on-site research and observation of the productions in London, Bayreuth, and Geneva were made significantly easier and more agreeable by the assistance of many people. In Bayreuth, the head of the Bayreuth Festspiele, Wolfgang Wagner, and his staff, especially Dr. Hardtmut Bauer and Gabrielle Taut, were very accommodating, as was Dr. Manfried Äger of the Richard Wagner–Gedenkstätte. I am grateful for permission to use photographs and drawings of the Bayreuth productions. In London my work was aided by the cooperation of William Bundy and members of the technical staff at Covent Garden: Fred Carro, David Enraght, and Jill Talbot. Katharine Wilkinson and her press staff at Covent Garden graciously provided access to press clippings and photographs. In Geneva, Jean-Claude Riber, producer-director of the Grand Theatre, allowed me to observe final rehearsals and backstage operations. His staff were equally hospitable, and I wish to thank especially Gisela Copplestone and Robert Jordan.

A study of scenography would be almost pointless without illustrations. I am grateful to the photographers (some anonymous, others identified in the captions) whose work supplements the illustrations provided by Svoboda. My special thanks go to Group Three Photography, Ltd., of London and to Dr. Jaromír Svoboda of the National Theatre, Prague, for use of their work. I am deeply grateful for a State of New York Grant in Aid that helped defray reproduction expenses, as well as a grant from the Vice President for Research and Educational Development of the State University of New York at Albany, which enabled the use of colored illustrations.

In countless ways, at home and abroad, this project has been aided by the cooperation of my wife, Grayce, to whom my gratitude extends beyond thanks.

PART ONE   JOSEF SVOBODA AND RICHARD WAGNER

Figure 2. Svoboda in action during a master class in scenography. *Photograph by Jarka Burian.*

Chapter 1 Josef Svoboda

If *Der Ring des Nibelungen* is counted as four separate operas, Josef Svoboda has created the scenography for a Richard Wagner work sixteen times: *Tristan und Isolde* three times; *Der Fliegende Holländer*, *Tannhäuser*, and each of the *Ring* operas (*Das Rheingold*, *Die Walküre*, *Siegfried*, and *Götterdämmerung*) twice each; and *Die Meistersinger* once. The productions have been staged in Svoboda's native Czechoslovakia as well as in Germany, Switzerland, and England, beginning with a 1959 Prague production of *Der Fliegende Holländer* and including the most recent, a Prague production of *Der Meistersinger* in 1978.

A contemporary designer of world stature, a designer dedicated to the use of the latest instruments, methods, and materials available to theater production, Svoboda has confronted problems that have challenged generations of designers. In tracing the encounters of Svoboda with Wagner, we have the opportunity not only of comparing Svoboda's work with that of some notable predecessors but also of comparing Svoboda's work on Wagner with some of his own work on other plays and operas, even his several treatments of a single Wagner opera. By examining Svoboda's varied approaches toward this lim-

ited and celebrated body of works, we may also gain insight into the techniques and problems of contemporary scenography and the evolving state of its art, and perhaps into the creative process itself.

Svoboda believes that Wagner offers great opportunities for a designer:

The music is dramatic in itself. The individual motifs are consistent, and you can orient yourself readily in the drama. The situations are well prepared, and he characterizes his figures perfectly. Other composers have some of these characteristics, but Wagner has something else: he knew the theater well, even the technical side, and he took the stage aspects seriously—magical effects as well as other techniques.[1]

Asked whether he associated any particular design or scenographic principles with Wagner, Svoboda revealed his general approach to all productions, not only those of Wagner:

It's not a matter of certain specific means, approaches, or conventions and no others. These are determined by the general line of the opera itself, the attitude toward it, and the philosophical point of it assumed at a given time. If the opera is used to stress a certain message about society, this may mean a choice of specific devices or scenographic methods—and the creation of new principles or "laws" among them—in the context of the guiding idea. But if I do a Wagner opera with a director who doesn't have that distinct a point of view, then as a designer I must take into account all the given circumstances and talents of the production, and consider to what extent I can interpret the opera—not as a single point to be made but more generally in terms of its feelings, the associations it creates when you follow all of Wagner's indications in the score. And I try to cointerpret with the director, quite openly, but with a design method that has the rhythm of our time, the expressive means of our day—not with old-fashioned associations or forms but in ways that say today and yet are equivalent to Wagner in terms of his tonalities, the romanticism of his music, and so on. For instance, the dragon in *Siegfried*: you must find means that are not old-fashioned, that are more neutral.

Svoboda's creativity may be viewed as an extension or evolution of the major nonrealistic movements in Western theater of the last century. Svoboda is the heir of Adolphe Appia and Gordon Craig, of many aspects of futurism, constructivism, and the Bauhaus. His creative roots also drew from the work of his own countrymen, especially Antonin Heythum, E. F. Burian, and Frantisek Tröster. I have described these affinities in earlier publications,[2] and I shall limit myself here to a brief summary of his background and his distinctive characteristics.

More than half of Josef Svoboda's sixty-three years have been spent as a scenographer in professional theater. He has designed more than five hundred productions of drama and opera throughout the world. He has also functioned as the chief of technical operations in the several theaters that comprise the Czech National Theater in Prague, where he was responsible for administration, personnel, budgeting, and liaison with government ministries. Trained as an architect, for the last twelve years Svoboda has been a professor of architecture in the Prague Academy of Fine and Industrial Arts, from which he himself graduated in 1950. In 1968 he received the title of National Artist in Czechoslovakia. He has exhibited abroad in England, France, Poland, and the United States, won major prizes in architecture as well as scenography (the Sikkens Prize in architecture from the Netherlands; gold medals at São Paolo, Brussels, and Montreal), received honorary degrees (London's Royal College of Art, Dennison University in Ohio), and been cited by international theater organizations for his distinctive work (the International Organization of Scenographers and Theater Technicians, and the American Theater Association).

Svoboda prefers the term *scenographer* to *scene de-*

signer because the scene designer has traditionally been associated with easel painting, with the creation of backgrounds and decoration, whereas the scenographer is concerned with all possible means of bringing a script to life on stage and expressing a production concept. A scenographer, moreover, is likely to be more an architect than a painter. He takes into account not only the space of the stage but its relation to the total theater space; not only painted decor but sound and lighting, including projections; not only static scenery but its potential for expressive movement. Science and technology are not alien mysteries to a scenographer but sources of enriched stage performance. They expand the spectrum of theater art.

For Svoboda, a fundamental premise underlies the uses of scenography: scenery, or, better, the total stage environment, does not merely establish a passive "place" for the dramatic action but provides a flexible, dynamic element of the total theatrical creation, an element capable of expressing the meanings of a play with a force equal to, or sometimes greater than, the spoken or mimed parts of the performance. Scenography, as Svoboda has often said, is an "actor" in the production, one whose performance may be a dominant expressive force or may form nothing more than a muted background. Like the actor, the scenography must be capable of transformation during the performance in response to the flow of the action, whether directly by material kinetics or indirectly by lighting, projections, or special devices (mirrors, for example).

Accompanying even the most extreme applications of this approach is Svoboda's cultivated sense of pure design, primarily in spatial relations but also in color, texture, and line. Closely related to this sense is his intuitive responsiveness to what he calls the "inner rhythms" of a work: the implicit, subtle configurations of imagery, tone, and variable intensities that create the core identity of a piece, under its overt or paraphrasable meanings. In embodying his sense of these rhythms in the final stage creation, Svoboda most often seeks a relatively abstract, metaphoric expression. It is not that he rejects realism as valid for certain works but that he prefers elimination of literal detail and fanciful decoration in favor of highly selective, figurative, and dramatically functional forms. "More important than having a door here or a window there is the creation of expressive spatial proportions."

Svoboda describes his creative process as the search

for the scenographic "system" that will most fully convey a play's meanings, as interpreted by the designer and the director. The system may be a fundamentally architectonic one, a structure of three-dimensional forms; or it may be based on special combinations of lighting and scrims, projections and strung cords, mirrors, kinetics, or other scenographic elements and methods. Whatever the system, its final form will be determined by considerations of both function and design, and it will reflect a contemporary sensibility rather than merely echo past traditions. In Svoboda's case the ultimate goal is the achievement of a scenographic *instrument* that offers the greatest opportunities for the expression of the central production concept:

It becomes a question of style: not style as external surface or manner but style as a way of thinking. We should ask ourselves why we use this or that technique, material, or device. Our purpose should be evident, and—most important—it should be clear that these means are being used by people today.

In Svoboda we find a rare combination: a highly gifted visual artist, a stage designer who commands a wide range of scientific and technological innovations, and an eminently practical man of the theater for whom the pressures of deadlines and collaborators are positive stimuli rather than disturbances. It is not that Svoboda is peerless in any one of these functions but that he is exceptionally strong in all three.

By the same token, it is not that every Svoboda work is a masterpiece, a model, an unqualified success. The blending and integration of scenographic elements are sometimes flawed or incompletely consummated; disproportions may occur; a concern with a certain effect or technique may distract from the overall harmony. Considering the many possibilities for problems—a miscalculation on the designer's part, a flaw in technical procedures, an eleventh-hour disagreement or misunderstanding among director, designer, and conductor—the generally high level of achievement of the leading theaters and opera houses is remarkable. In Svoboda's case, the record is all the more impressive in view of his often unorthodox, risk-taking, innovative approaches. A man who places enormous value on precision and mastery of craftsmanship, who abhors dilettantism, and who steeps himself in the background of the pieces on which he works, Svoboda nonetheless describes himself as "something of a gambler or sharpshooter. After all the research and discussion, you have to take chances and follow your instincts."

Svoboda's candid admission calls attention to what is perhaps an indispensable talent of all artists—an instinctual response to the very "scent" of the thing at hand. In one of the twentieth century's most influential works of theater theory, *The Idea of a Theatre*, Francis Fergusson repeatedly refers to this talent as "histrionic sensibility" and identifies it as the essence of the creative act of theater. It is "the mimetic perception of action"; "a primitive and direct awareness . . . of things and people 'before predication'"; it involves "a sympathetic response of the whole psyche."[3] In Svoboda's case it is a talent that he has disciplined and made a fruitful part of a creative process by yoking it to a painstaking command of the materials and techniques of his craft.

A final and characteristic aspect of that creative process is Svoboda's staying with certain materials, techniques, or, perhaps, certain abstract forms (for example, cube, ellipse, spiral, intersecting planes) until he has discovered within them as many of their potential values and applications as possible. The results may manifest themselves in several productions within a given season or may recur only after years, for Svoboda is reluctant to employ any material, technique, or form unless it is warranted by a specific script or production concept. This habitual practice of Svoboda, which testifies to his persistence as well as his ready imagination, underlies some of his most striking work and will be evident in examining the variety of his scenography for Wagner.

Chapter 2 The Staging of Wagner's Operas

Passionate feelings and controversy have swirled around Wagner, his works, and his ideas almost since he first came to public attention. Becoming very nearly a cult figure in the late nineteenth century, Wagner continues to arouse extremes of adulation and antipathy. There are few today who would deny his genius as a composer of music dramas, but many who still associate him not only with an excessive, perhaps morbid romanticism but with fascism. Many of the fascist associations are no doubt unfair, the result of Hitler's identification of many of his own ideals with those he found in Wagner's works and writings and his lavish patronage of the Bayreuth Festival as an official showcase of the Nazi regime. At the same time, however, it is not too difficult to read fascist overtones in Wagner's preoccupations with racial purity, idealizations of sacrifice to higher authority, and mystical intoxication with death.

But this is not a study of Wagner the man or of Wagner's sociopolitical role. These brief observations are mentioned only because the accusations indicate the complexity of his reputation, a reputation that has probably been present, if only peripherally, in the minds of those who have produced and criticized his works.

More to the point in a study of the staging of Wagner

is that many of his ideas about theater art and the production of his own works, as well as the critical responses to those ideas, have influenced production theory and practice down to our own day. Wagner has come to be identified with a form of theater that employs multiple artistic strategies to produce an essentially uncritical, emotive, at times mystical response in the audience. Central to his theory and production practice was his ideal of the *Gesamtkunstwerk*, the collective or total work of art in which all elements of production unite in an ideal, balanced fusion of auditory and visual stimuli in order to create an appeal to the total emotional range of the spectator. Wagner's legendary, mythical subject matter, his leitmotifs and continuous melodic line, his illusionistic staging, and even his architectural innovations (an invisible orchestra pit and a double proscenium arch to create a "mystic gulf" between stage and audience) were all designed to promote a powerfully emotive, if not irrational, experience.

The Gesamtkunstwerk ideal has been challenged on two main counts. On the theoretical or aesthetic level, the very possibility of a truly combined work of art has been questioned. Suzanne Langer has argued that in practice one art ultimately dominates another. Dance usually dominates music, music subordinates words, and drama on stage usually overwhelms painting, sculpture, or architecture. As Langer says, "There are no happy marriages in art—only successful rape."[1] On the more practical level of audience response, assuming the Gesamtkunstwerk ideal were possible to realize, many critics, most notably Bertolt Brecht, have argued against its desirability.[2] Theater, they believe, ought to encourage in audiences not a primarily emotional, noncritical response to human experience but quite the opposite—an alert, questioning, at least partially detached view of the performance and its relevance to the world of the audience.

What emerges from these disputes regarding theory and practice? Whether or not some of Wagner's special theories about his works possess demonstrable aesthetic validity, and whether or not one approves of the effect of his works in performance, it is difficult to deny the powerful appeal of their distinctive union of music and drama. For Wagner that union resulted from his efforts to increase the significance of the opera's *dramatic* component: "The error in the art-genre of opera consists herein:—*that a means of Expression (Music) has been made the end, while the End of Expression (the Drama) has been made a means.*"[3] It is ironic that most poeple have come to reject his basic premise that the point of opera is drama, affirming instead that the ultimate value of opera is the music, a view common in opera criticism. The argument is perhaps a futile one and creates an artificial conflict of absolutes—music *or* drama. More important is that operas, Wagner's above all, involve a special integration of both elements and thus provide the unique excitement and challenge that confront all who stage these works.

Identifying exactly what places Wagner's operas at the summit of music-in-theater is not easy. Of enormous significance, of course, was Wagner's writing of his own librettos, which allowed him to express his dramatically oriented creativity. The great music critic Ernest Newman, not an unqualified admirer of Wagner, explained the composer's inimitable and unapproachable qualities:

Wagner's mind is simply that of the ordinary opera-composer pushed to its logical extreme. Instead of being spasmodically dramatic, it is dramatic from start to finish; . . . Wagner is able to conceive in musical phrases *all* characters, *all* episodes, *all* the internal play of force upon force.[4]

Many of these issues surrounding Wagner, his works, and his ideas involve a number of fundamental aesthetic questions of theater staging in general (for example, the relative importance of the several components of a production). A more specific, and for this study central, question is the relation of design or scenography to total staging. No better example of the kind of problem that inheres in these issues is likely to be found than the candid admission of George Bernard Shaw after witnessing an early production of *Der Ring des Nibelungen* at Bayreuth itself:

One had to admit at Bayreuth that here was the utmost perfection of the pictorial stage, and that its machinery could go no further. Nevertheless, having seen it at its best, fresh from Wagner's own influence, I must also admit that my favorite way of enjoying a performance of *The Ring* is to sit at the back of a box, comfortable on two chairs, feet up, and listen without looking. The truth is, a man whose imagination cannot serve him better than the most costly devices of the imitative scenepainter, should not go to the theater, and as a matter of fact does not.[5]

To "listen without looking": much the same has been said about performances of Shakespeare or, perhaps even more disturbingly, about theater performance as such.

Some people prefer to read Shakespeare at home rather than to see his plays in performance. The principle is the same for Shakespeare or Wagner, and it may be traced back to Aristotle's relegation of "spectacle" to last place in his ranking of the six elements of tragic drama. It involves a fundamental question underlying all subsequent questions and theories of theater production: Why *stage* a play or opera at all?

The argument usually concerns plays or operas in which the text or music is of notable value, so much so that the *staging* of the text is seen as peripheral at best, or as outright distortion of the literary or musical values at worst. To say that there is simply a strong tradition or habit of staging such works is undoubtedly true but may not be sufficient justification. Perhaps the fundamental point is that Wagner (and others) deliberately and painstakingly wrought his works with staging in mind as an intrinsic, organic part of his total creation. It is not too much to say that the music itself must have been influenced by his sense of its performance in conjunction with, or as part of, an enactment occurring on stage before an audience. To an appreciable degree the music was shaped with a sense of time, space, and movement conditioned by the composer's awareness of its final role as one element (granted, the paramount element) in a complex *Gestalt* of words, ideas, tones, rhythms, colors, movements, tableaux, scenic representations, lighting, and so on. Ignoring or dismissing all staging limits, indeed distorts, what Wagner created. He did not merely write superb, dramatic music. He wrote music dramas. And dramas of whatever kind imply staging as a vital, inherent aspect of their total identity.

Questions of what *kind* of staging are another matter. Like Shaw, one may prefer one's own imagination or an alternative approach to a particular staging. Shaw referred disparagingly to "the imitative scenepainter." Would he have also objected to a less stereotyped scenography?

If one grants that there is not only justification for staging but also a genuine need for it, what sort of staging shall it be? Shall it follow Wagner's original staging? That is, shall it be a form of romantic realism, observing the trappings of Nordic mythology? Or shall it not only use modern techniques but also reject any fidelity to Wagner's original staging or even to a simplified version of the mythological, quasihistorical eras of

the text and stage directions? How many liberties can be taken?

There is a not inconsiderable body of Wagnerian performers, students, and critics who take the conservative position that Wagner's original ideas and stage directions should be preserved, allowing for certain modifications of style and technique. They see no gain in radical departures from the original, maintaining that such departures are in fact counterproductive distortions with little more than ephemeral shock value. Wagner's widow, Cosima, for example, felt that the original creation possessed a certain artistic sanctity and that the function of subsequent artists was essentially that of expert servants, loyal to the prototype: "The *Ring* was produced here in 1876, and therefore there is nothing more to be discovered in the field of scenery and production."[6]

Opposition to this view has taken two forms. One, most notably represented by Adolphe Appia, asserts that Wagner's original staging was inappropriate, that his approach was misconceived from the beginning.[7] The other is perhaps willing to grant that Wagner's own staging may have been effective enough in its time but that subsequent revivals must violate the prototype in

Figure 3. The 1896 setting for scene 2 of *Das Rheingold* at Bayreuth, designed by Max Brückner. The two-dimensional painted scenery of this period was intended to provide a natural background. Such settings endured virtually unchanged for decades. *Photograph by permission of Festspiele Bayreuth.*

Figure 4. Wagner's setting for act 3 of the original production of *Die Walküre* at Bayreuth, 1876. *Photograph by permission of Festspiele Bayreuth.*

order to be true to its spirit. This attitude is best expressed by Ortega y Gasset's remarks about Goethe:

There is but one way left to save a classic: to give up revering him and use him for our own salvation—that is, lay aside his classicism, to bring him close to us, to make him contemporary, to set his pulse going again with an injection of blood from our own veins, whose ingredients are *our* passions . . . and our problems.[8]

For some fifty years after the initial productions at Bayreuth, Wagner's original staging dominated the revivals of his works. What was that staging like? A form of late nineteenth-century romantic realism, it consisted of elaborate settings built up of layers of two-dimensional painted scenery leading to a painted backdrop (figs. 3–6). It was romantic in its idealization and intensification of subject matter, in its indulgence in the exotic and ornate. It was realistic in that it went to great pains to provide naturalistically detailed indications of place and a feeling of authenticity, even when the locale being depicted existed only in myth or legend. The stage was usually filled with objects, somewhat like a cluttered, overstuffed Victorian bourgeois interior; everything was intended to seem real, even the most magical and mystical of Wagner's scenarios.

Although Wagner said relatively little on the subject of scenery, and what he did say was often contradictory, the main tendencies of his thinking were clear. As the noted theater historian Alois Nagler pointed out, "The painted stage of illusion was his domain, and he never demanded more (or less, for that matter) of the scenic artist than his painterly illusionism was able to achieve on the stage."[9] Wagner himself said, "As the final and most complete means of expression in visual art, landscape painting will become the life-giving soul of the whole construction. It will teach us to build for the drama the stage on which it will itself represent the warm natural background for the living actor."[10]

The inconsistencies in Wagner's own thinking are evident when we compare his remarks calling for an unobtrusive accompaniment to the dramatic action with other statements indicating his fascination with stage machinery and melodramatic theatrical effects, many of which dated back to baroque spectacles. On the one hand, he could say, "I am only striving for . . . a certain poetic effect, but no theatrical pomp. . . . I want only a subdued background to characterize a dramatic situation."[11] On the other hand, the stage directions at the end of *Götterdämmerung* call for Brünnhilde's self-

Figure 5. The original 1876 staging of *Götterdämmerung*, showing the Gibichung Hall in act 1, scene 2. *Photograph by permission of Festspiele Bayreuth.*

Figure 6. The first production of *Tristan und Isolde* at Bayreuth in 1886, act 3, designed by Max Brückner. *Photograph by permission of Richard Wagner-Gedenkstätte, Bayreuth.*

immolation with her horse on a funeral pyre, the burning and collapse of a palace, the overflowing of the Rhine River, Rhine maidens swimming on a wave over the pyre, and in the distance the burning of Valhalla itself.

Geoffrey Skelton in his excellent study *Wagner at Bayreuth* has suggested that Wagner intended his stage directions as "a help to the reader's imagination [rather] than . . . a practical guide to the producer."[12] Others, like Walter Panofsky, have noted that Wagner seemed trapped and frustrated by the conventions and techniques of his time, undeniably fascinated by the sheer element of "show," but also bitterly disappointed by the discrepancies between his visions and the impossibility of his stage to embody them.[13] He is known to have regretted his excessive attention to old theatrical conventions, once saying, "How I abhor all these costumes and paint! . . . Now that I have made the orchestra invisible, I should like to invent an invisible stage."[14]

Nevertheless, this was only an isolated cry of frustration. The sheer inertia of the stage traditions of his day prevailed during Wagner's lifetime and long after his death, especially as enforced by Wagner's widow and only slightly modified by his son Siegfried. Only after World War I did the scenery at Bayreuth begin to acquire

three dimensions, and not until the late 1920s did optical projections begin to be used for more than incidental background effects. In retrospect it is perhaps surprising that it took so long for advances in design and techniques—the so-called New Stagecraft—to be applied to Wagner, especially at Bayreuth, but it is a testimonial to the strength of the original Wagner tradition and to the fidelity of his family and his artistic descendants, who maintained what they regarded as the authentic Wagner style.

Not that opposition did not soon appear, most significantly in the revolutionary ideas of Adolphe Appia, a fervent devotee of Wagner's works who was very disturbed by the internal contradictions in the staging of the operas at Bayreuth in the late 1880s. Appia, whose ideas may be related to the profound counternaturalistic tendencies of the symbolists, was appalled by the inconsistency, if not antagonism, between the magnificently evocative powers of the music, along with the enactment of the drama, and what seemed to him to be totally inappropriate, inadequate staging and scenery, particularly as evident in the inexpressive lighting, the artifice of painted canvas and papier-mâché, and many other tired theatrical conventions, none of which corre-

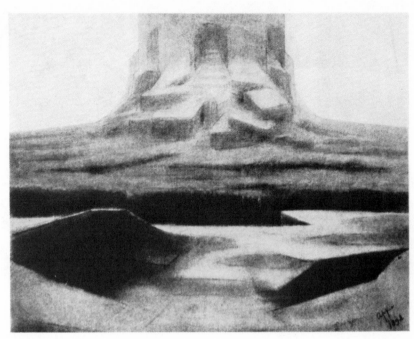

Figure 7. Adolphe Appia's 1892 design for scene 2 of *Das Rheingold*. A comparison with figure 3 makes clear the vast gulf separating Appia's artistic vision from that of his contemporaries. *By permission of Adolphe Appia Foundation, Bern.*

sponded to the music's power to reveal "the hidden world of our inner life."[15]

Appia developed his criticisms and proposals in a number of writings, chiefly *La mise en scène du drame wagnérien* (1895) and *Die Muzik und die Inscenierung* (1899).[16] His ideas were many and sometimes complexly expressed, but his innovations may be summarized briefly. At the heart of his reform was his insistence that the external staging be based on the internal qualities of the music rather than on the graphic indications of the stage directions. Moreover, the staging should be radically simplified and should subordinate painted scenery in favor of relatively abstract, three-dimensional forms that combine suggestiveness and symbolic values with maximum opportunities for rhythmically expressive tableaux and movement by the performers. Rejecting a stage that was essentially two-dimensional, Appia envisioned the stage as a volume of space in which plastic forms are organized in rhythmic configurations related to the music and the movement of the performers (figs. 7–10). The culminating element that unified the entire scene was lighting, lighting that would be infinitely flexible, designed to stress the plasticity of the total composition and to respond to the

musical score. "Light is to production what music is to the score: the expressive element in opposition to literal signs; and, like music, light can express only what belongs to the 'inner essence of all vision.'"[17]

Appia's attempts to base the staging of Wagner's operas on the subjective, emotive state of the music and the feelings of the characters (the one essentially synonymous with the other) are really the primary source of most subsequent departures from the original Bayreuth pattern. It is ironic that Appia's proposals, rejected by Cosima Wagner in the 1890s, came to influence the work of other Wagnerian producers and designers (for example, Oskar Strnad and Alfred Roller in Vienna) in the early years of the new century before Appia himself had the opportunity of designing a Wagner production. Appia's own first production did not occur until the 1923–24 season at La Scala in Milan, when Arturo Toscanini invited him to stage *Tristan und Isolde*. Even at that late date, Appia's methods were considered too stark and unorthodox by many, perhaps partly because his ideas and designs had become even more austere and less representational as a result of his work with Jacques Dalcroze and the latter's projects in eurythmics. More controversy greeted his staging of *Das Rheingold*

and *Die Walküre* in Basel the following season. So great was the disturbance in response to Appia's abstract blocks, steps, and drapes that the succeeding two operas of the *Ring*, *Siegfried* and *Götterdämmerung*, were never staged.

Appia's influence was partially evident in the productions at Bayreuth in the 1930s, which were staged under the leadership of Heinz Tietjen and his designer, Emil Preetorius. Much of the quasirealistic painted detail was scrapped in favor of simpler forms and expressive lighting in order to reflect the music more faithfully (figs. 11, 12). Tietjen summed up their efforts: "We sought to evolve a stage setting which restricted the use of objects to essentials and gave the main role to the adaptable and highly visual instrument of lighting."[18] Nevertheless, Preetorius and Tietjen were not prepared to go as far as Appia or to abandon the realistic, natural foundations of staging they felt essential to Wagner's works, as Preetorius's remarks reveal: "The possibility of a fully free embodiment of the visual, of a basically new approach in the direction of simplification, of bare symbolism is only applicable to Wagner to a very limited extent if one is not to obscure the basic idea of his work."[19]

Not until after World War II did the reforms proposed by Appia bear full fruit, appropriately and yet ironically in the productions of Wagner's grandsons, Wieland and Wolfgang, in the shrine at Bayreuth itself. They were the inheritors not only of the spirit of Appia but of subsequent twentieth-century movements in art and theater, and they were sufficiently detached from the original Wagner traditions to feel free to make radical departures from the models of the past (figs. 13–15). They were, moreover, prompted by the severe limitations of the postwar economy and by a desire to dissociate Wagner and Bayreuth from the Nazi ties of the 1930s and early 1940s. Wieland Wagner started with a virtually bare stage and permitted only an absolute minimum of abstract, symbolic elements of construction and lighting to suggest the mood of each scene. He explained, "If one wants to build a new house, one must first dig up the ground in which the foundations are to be laid. . . .[We are concerned] to seek out the inner laws inherent in a work of genius and to interpret it uncompromisingly, as we find it mirrored in our own souls."[20]

Geoffrey Skelton points out that Wolfgang was the more practical and functional in his approach and included more realistic elements, whereas Wieland was

Figure 11. A 1936 Bayreuth production of *Die Walküre*, act 3, designed by Emil Preetorius under the artistic direction of Heinz Tietjen. By 1936 Bayreuth had approached Appia's designs of the 1890s but was not yet ready for the Appia of the 1920s; see figures 9 and 10. *Photograph by permission of Festspiele Bayreuth.*

Figure 12. Siegfried discovers Brünnhilde in act 3, scene 2, of *Siegfried* in the 1937 Preetorius-Tietjen production at Bayreuth. *Photograph by permission of Festspiele Bayreuth.*

the more visionary and extreme in rejecting such traces of the past. The productions of both, however, reduced the stage picture to elemental, stark forms and made full use of modern equipment and techniques in lighting to accompany and reinforce the music dramas. Their work was a fulfillment of numerous tendencies in modern art, above all those of nonrepresentational abstraction and symbolism, in striving to arrive at the inner essence of a work. They followed farthest the road that Appia originally laid out, farther perhaps than Appia himself might have gone. Their productions were the ultimate embodiment of a spirit articulated by the American designer Lee Simonson a few years before Wagner's grandsons began producing at Bayreuth:

The poetry and power of Wagner's vision reside in his general picture . . . rather than in its specific details, often cumbersome, dramatically clumsy, and technically not worth . . . the time and effort involved. . . . *The Ring* can best be dramatized for a contemporary audience in a tradition of scenic design which Wagner neither knew nor really conceived.[21]

As could have been anticipated, the "new" Bayreuth created a furor in opera circles. Accusations of heresy alternated with enthusiastic support for the daring innovations. Those championing the new productions claimed that they succeeded in eliminating archaic conventions that were anomalies in a modern opera theater, that they allowed the music, especially that of the orchestra, to make its most expressive contribution, and that they revealed the elemental, mythical level of the music dramas more completely than had the more traditional staging. The antagonists stressed that the lyrical, romantic roots of the operas required comparable staging, leaving moot the complex question of what "romantic" and "lyrical" really mean. Is a fur- and armor-covered Siegfried in a forest of painted flats more romantic and lyrical than one isolated in a pool of light on a bare circular platform against an abstract green and yellow cyclorama projection? The roots of the problem lie deep. Alois Nagler saw in the neo-Bayreuth productions a reflection of the twentieth-century evolution of the scenic oratorio, whereas Wagner's operas had their foundation in the tradition of mimetic drama, with its more overt, fuller, emotive stage depiction. Nagler concluded, "Richard Wagner must not end his dramatic career in the Bauhaus or in some other tomb of allegorical abstraction."[22] And so the arguments have continued.

There is no way of staging Wagner that is likely to satisfy everyone. What is brilliant to one critic or spec-

Figure 14. Wieland Wagner's 1952 *Tristan*, act 3, at Bayreuth.
Compare with figures 6 and 10. Bayreuth's new depiction of the
scene suggests the extent to which Wagner's grandsons reduced
scenery to a minimum while retaining a suggestion of place and
atmosphere. *Photograph by permission of Festspiele Bayreuth.*

Figure 15. The Wolfgang Wagner *Siegfried*, act 3, scene 2, at Bayreuth in 1964. A comparison with the 1937 Preetorius-Tietjen production (fig. 12) demonstrates how sharp was the break from traditional Bayreuth staging. *Photograph by permission of Festspiele Bayreuth.*

tator is outrageous or laughable to another; what is authentic to a third will be hopelessly uninventive to a fourth. What remains constant is the search for interpretations and forms that will satisfy the creative drives of those responsible for the productions, maintain fidelity to the spirit of Wagner's originals, and also speak with authority and freshness to today's audiences. The neo-Bayreuth productions of Wagner's grandsons did not merely establish a single extreme break with the past; they also set a clear precedent for a variety of notable experiments in staging and of startling innovations in the interpretation of Wagner's themes.

Two major characteristics mark most of the productions that have progressed beyond Bayreuth of the 1950s and 1960s (that is, beyond the work of Wieland and Wolfgang Wagner). The first is an extreme reinterpretation of the traditional themes and philosophic overtones of the operas, including explicit dislocations in the place and period of the settings. Examples are *Ring* productions at Kassel (1970–74), which placed the action in a futuristic space age, and at Leipzig (1973–76) and Bayreuth (1976), in both of which the action was divided between the nineteenth century and today. In these productions computer control rooms and neon rainbows,

hydroelectric dams, turbines and boiler rooms, New York City skylines, and modernistic interior decor shifted the operas' emphases from myth and magic to contemporary socioeconomic comment. The second major characteristic is a notable concern for the form of the presentations, for innovations in staging in an attempt to extend the parameters of the art of theater while presenting an essentially recognizable Wagner. Svoboda has been primarily associated with productions of this second kind; that is, his scenography for Wagner's operas demonstrates a consolidation of some of his earlier work and also a movement toward still newer forms of scenic expression and the technical innovations to achieve those forms.

Figure 18. The act 2 interior scene of the Prague production. *Photograph by Jaromír Svoboda.*

Figure 19. The farewell scene in act 3 of the Prague production. *Photograph by Jaromír Svoboda.*

Der Fliegende Holländer   25

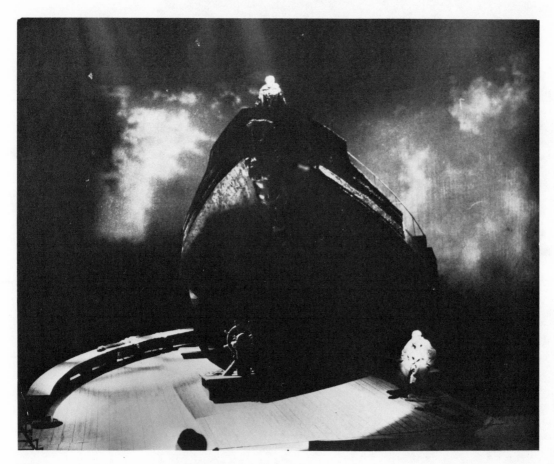

Figure 20. The Dutchman's boat in its dominant position after
swinging up and over Daland's boat in act 1 of the Bayreuth
Holländer in 1969.

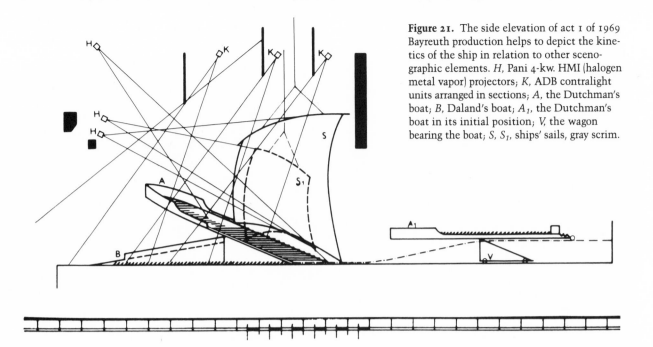

Figure 21. The side elevation of act 1 of 1969 Bayreuth production helps to depict the kinetics of the ship in relation to other scenographic elements. *H*, Pani 4-kw. HMI (halogen metal vapor) projectors; *K*, ADB contralight units arranged in sections; *A*, the Dutchman's boat; *B*, Daland's boat; A_1, the Dutchman's boat in its initial position; *V,* the wagon bearing the boat; *S*, S_1, ships' sails, gray scrim.

forming the central, monumental dramatic image. Deliberately avoiding the naturalistic detail of cliffs, shore, and village port indicated in the stage directions, the scenography consisted of a unit set (a basic set which, with minor variations, can function for several locations), with the rear of Daland's boat as the chief element. Besides functioning as a boat in acts 1 and 3, it also formed the space for the spinning room interior of the second act, thus eliminating the three different sets of the Prague production and enabling the opera to be played without a pause and without a curtain. The multiple scrims and other projection surfaces of the Prague production were almost entirely scrapped. All that remained were two abstract sails of scrim above the boat to register abstract filmed projections of both clouds and waves, but this was simply a supplementary, secondary feature in relation to the architectonic forms of the boats (fig. 20).

The Dutchman's boat was part of this unit set for all but the very beginning and end of the opera. Its initial dramatic appearance was handled in much the same way as in Prague, but with perhaps more effectiveness because of the greater depth of the Bayreuth stage and its technically more advanced facilities. The ghostship itself was larger (some fifty feet—or fifteen meters —long), and its bottom contained a scrim, which provided the audience with a dramatic vision of the imprisoned ghost crew at their benches. In its position above the deck of Daland's boat, the prow lifted the Dutchman more than twenty feet high (figs. 21–23). In the second act, the boat remained on stage, towering over Daland's boat, but suitably disguised by lighting and an arrangement of netting similar to that of the Prague production (fig. 24). This second act especially pleased Svoboda in its suggestion of the heroine's capture within the nets, as well as her tendency to mix dream and reality. The Dutchman's large portrait hung above the doorway, which in turn was just below the darkened prow of his boat, thereby producing another strong moment in the opera when the Dutchman himself appears to Senta from the prow of his boat.

August Everding, the director of the Bayreuth production, underlined the significance of the scenography of the first two acts:

The approach of the ship was not to be a mere optical trick, but to exhibit the existential menace experienced by the steerman. Here came not merely something dangerous but rather something numinous, like the Wandering Jew. The spinning room

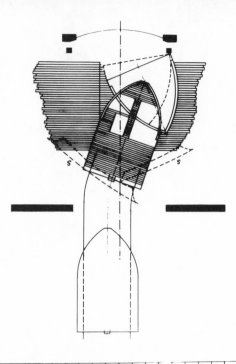

Figure 22. The ground plan for act 1 of 1969 Bayreuth production, showing the path of the ghostship's movement up and over Daland's boat: *S*, the simplified scrim sails used for projections of sea and clouds.

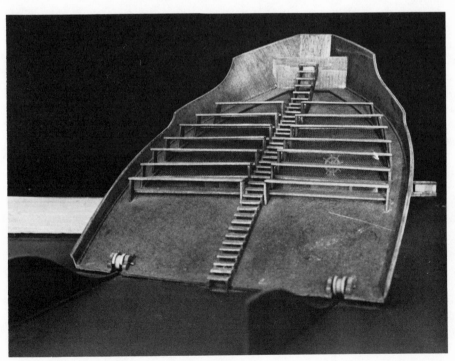

Figure 23. The model of the Dutchman's boat in the Bayreuth production as seen from the rear. Several elements are evident: the benches for the imprisoned ghost crew, the stairs for the first dramatic entrance of the Dutchman at the peak of the prow, the wheels and rails that enabled the ship to move from a horizontal to an inclined position, and the partially scrimmed undersurface of the boat that made the ghost crew visible.

Figure 24. For act 2 of the Bayreuth *Holländer* the boats remained in position but were converted into the setting for the sewing room, chiefly by the use of stylized fishnets and carefully controlled atmospheric lighting (both of which were very similar to the Prague scenography—see figure 18).

Figure 25. For the act 3 harbor scene at Bayreuth a few properties and a segment of bleachers for the festive chorus were added. Projections of clouds may be seen on the stylized sails.

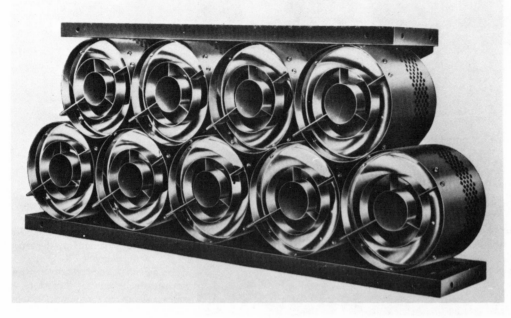

Figure 26. A bank or section of contralight units; see note 4.

was not to have any solid beams or boards, but instead the transitoriness of the entire piece was to be effected by the construction of nets that Svoboda provided.[2]

The third act retained the two boats and added a set of stairs or bleachers to accommodate the chorus of festive townspeople and to provide an elevated point from which Senta leaps into the sea (fig. 25). The culminating moment depicting the mystic union of Senta and the Dutchman above the waves in which his ship has sunk was a problem not successfully resolved. Svoboda's original idea was to have the lovers represented by two brilliant lights that approach each other (actually reflections from a large parabolic mirror), increasing in intensity until the audience is temporarily blinded at the moment the opera ends; by the time its sight is adjusted, everything has disappeared, an effect similar to one Svoboda had used for the ending of Karl Orff's *Prometheus* (Munich, 1968) and B. A. Zimmermann's *Die Soldaten* (Munich, 1969).[3] In this case, technical problems intervened and an alternative solution was attempted. The figures of the two lovers were to appear behind a very strong contralight (fig. 26),[4] elevated as if walking above the sea, but shortness of time prevented

that approach from being perfected, and only the light remained. Nevertheless, both Svoboda and Everding still felt that the idea of presenting a vision of the two lovers was sound. Svoboda has said that he would prefer working out the contralight method with doubles for the two lovers elevated behind the contralight, to be seen as if behind a scrim, a scenographic treatment that became part of Svoboda's original concept for the Bayreuth production of *Tristan* some five years later.

The two productions of *Der Fliegende Holländer*, although separated by ten years, were marked by Svoboda's characteristic rejection of a naturalistic, pictorial approach in favor of an architectonic, functional scenography that selects one or two crucial elements from the world of the libretto (in this case, the boats), presents them in a simplified, partially abstract manner, and integrates them with one or two other scenographic systems, such as the lighting and projections in these productions, which, in conjunction with netting, scrim, or canvas, created a distinctive, neoromantic atmosphere.

Chapter 4 *Tannhäuser*

In considering *Tannhäuser* we again find Svoboda designing two different productions with a number of similar elements: Hamburg in 1969 and London in 1973. Written in 1842–45, shortly after *Der Fliegende Holländer*, *Tannhäuser* is regarded by critics as the first opera to show signs of Wagner's more mature artistry. The drama concerns the minstrel-knight Tannhäuser's inner struggle between sensual and spiritual love, as embodied in his relation to Venus and to Elizabeth. The spiritual force of Elizabeth ultimately prevails but not until after Tannhäuser's severe penance and Elizabeth's death. Having achieved atonement and salvation, Tannhäuser himself dies.

Wagner devotes one entire scene to the depiction of the erotic enchantment by which Venus holds Tannhäuser in thrall, and her presence is felt in subsequent scenes as well. This first scene begins in the medieval Venusberg, in a cavelike grotto where the goddess, according to legend, has maintained her dominion. At the end of the scene, by which time Tannhäuser has renounced Venus and declared his need for penance and the help of the Virgin Mary, a sudden transformation occurs: without leaving his position, Tannhäuser finds himself in the wooded valley of the Wartburg.

Perhaps the chief problem for a designer is finding a visual image for the Venusberg scene. The grotto has been depicted in countless ways, ranging from a dreamlike vision to a riotous bacchanal, from the cluttered pseudonaturalism of the earliest productions to the severe abstraction of Wieland Wagner. Related scenographic problems are the virtually instantaneous shift from the Venusberg to the valley and the visual echoes of the Venusberg element in subsequent scenes.

Svoboda responded to these challenges with a nonrealistic, abstract approach based on a permanent architectonic ground plan and an ingenious combination of a system of projections and a system of mirrors. The combination operated in both productions but with interesting variations, once again demonstrating Svoboda's characteristic pursuit of certain techniques until he is satisfied that he has extracted from them a variety of effective applications.

Neither projections nor mirrors were new to Svoboda's work. Early forms of the projection techniques evident in the Prague *Fliegende Holländer* could later be seen in his complex audiovisual display of Emil Radok's *Diapolyekran* at Expo '67 in Montreal and in his traditional theater production of Richard Strauss's *Frau ohne Schat-*

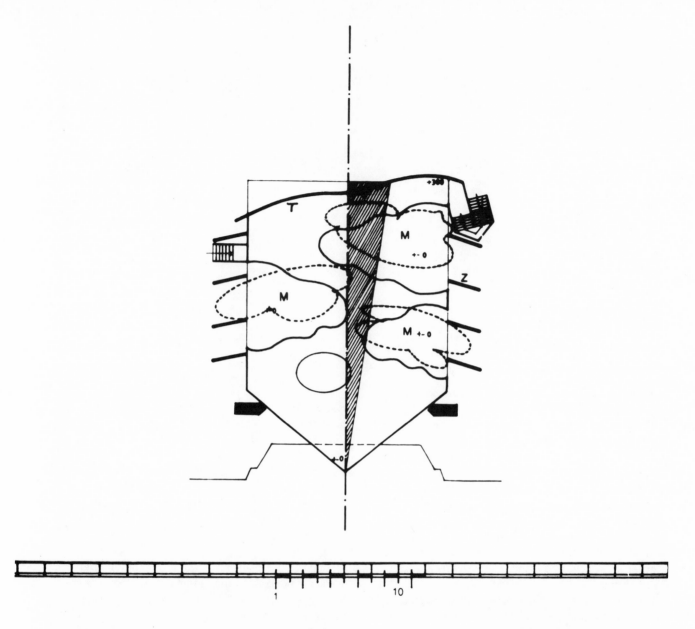

Figure 27. Ground plan of act 1 of 1969 Hamburg *Tannhäuser:* M, mirrors suspended over the pockets adjacent to the inclined pathway; Z, black velvet masking legs; T, Studio folio for rear projections.

Figure 28. Act 1, scene 1. The effect of multiple images for the Venusberg scene in the Hamburg *Tannhäuser* is best captured in the downstage-left mirror, which reflects a performer below stage as well as the image projected on the carpet around her; the mirror itself also serves as a projection surface for another set of images. The cyclorama took rear projections.

ten in London (1967). Svoboda's work with mirrors can be traced back to such productions as H. Zinner's *Devil's Circle* (Prague, 1955) and Mozart's *Die Zauberflöte* (Prague, 1961). The most direct ancestor of the combined technique, however, was the 1965 Prague production of Karel and Josef Capek's *Insect Comedy*, in which two large mirrors were tilted at different angles behind and over a large turntable, which was covered by ground cloths of different patterns. The result was a kaleidoscope of direct and reflected images reinforcing the impression of insects swarming. In the *Tannhäuser* productions Svoboda eliminated the turntable but added one fundamental element (as well as several refinements): the mirrored surfaces reflected not simply painted or three-dimensional objects but projected images.

THE HAMBURG PRODUCTION

The variety of projected and mirrored images in Svoboda's first *Tannhäuser*, at Hamburg in 1969, surpassed anything in his previous work. To depict the erotic, sensuous environment of the Venusberg grotto, Svoboda suspended mirrors in shapes clearly suggesting female

sexuality above a number of "pockets" formed by a jagged, elevated path that ran upstage from the edge of the stage apron and reached a height of some six feet toward the rear (fig. 27). Within these pockets prone performers mimed erotically suggestive, dancelike movements, which were of course reflected to the audience by the mirrors. But this was not all that was reflected. A battery of slide projectors cast equally suggestive, sensuous images and colors onto projection cloths lining the bottom of the pockets, onto the elevated path itself, onto the rear of a translucent cyclorama of Studio folio backing up the stage space,[1] onto the rear of the mirrors themselves (which had a projection cloth surface) in order to be reflected by the other mirrors, and onto the front of the mirrors as well, which were covered by scrim and therefore caught the projected images (fig. 28). The result was an enormous collage of projected colors and images perceived directly and by reflection and capable of considerable variation by altering the intensity of the general lighting and projections. With one exception, mirrors were employed in the first scene only. The second scene was based on projections only, and the third scene on lighting and architectural elements.

The instant transformation to the valley was handled

Figure 29. In both *Tannhäuser* productions, the valley of the Wartburg was created by projecting abstract patterns of foliage onto scrims lowered into the pockets formed by the elevated paths. Covent Garden production, act 1, scene 2, 1973. *Photograph by Group Three Photography, Ltd.*

Figure 30. A rehearsal photo of the Hamburg *Tannhäuser*, act 3, showing the superimposition of some of the Venusberg images on the basic projections of the forest in the valley of the Wartburg.

by flipping the mirrors so that their nonmirrored side faced the audience, lifting them out, and simultaneously lowering a series of special scrim panels of different widths that suggested tree trunks, onto which were projected abstract patterns of foliage (fig. 29). The third of the three settings, the interior of the Wartburg, maintained the same ground structure of the raked and elevated path but filled the openings with bleacherlike benches to accommodate the chorus and principals of the song contest (somewhat like the supplemental unit in the third act of *Der Fliegende Holländer* at Bayreuth). This third scene was completed scenographically by Svoboda's special contralighting system in conjunction with a two-dimensional Romanesque cornice that was silhouetted against the intense beams of low-voltage projectors hung high at the rear of the stage.

In the final scene, which returns to the valley, Tannhäuser once again experiences a vision of Venus. The effect was created by having one of the mirrors from the first scene reflect Venus and some dancers who were hidden in one of the cavities formed by the elevated path, as well as by using fleetingly some of the sensuous Venusberg images (fig. 30).

THE LONDON PRODUCTION

In the nearly four years between the two *Tannhäuser* productions Svoboda evolved still further refinements with projections, helped by technical advances in projection instruments and projection surfaces. He also began exploring the possibilities of still another scenographic principle or system, that of pneumatics, as applied to scenery, costumes, props, and, indeed, mirrors. Not all of the experiments were in fact used in productions, but his work on them extended the potential range of scenography.[2]

In two earlier productions Svoboda had increased the expressiveness of projections by multiplying the sheer number of projected images and by exploring the implications of additive color in the combined projections. The productions of Alexander Scriabin's *Prometheus* (Milan, 1972) and Igor Stravinsky's *Firebird* (Copenhagen, 1972) were marked by a far greater number of instruments and projection surfaces than usual and, correspondingly, by more complex cuing systems to orchestrate the projections and general lighting with the musical score. (The *Firebird* also used a large mirror

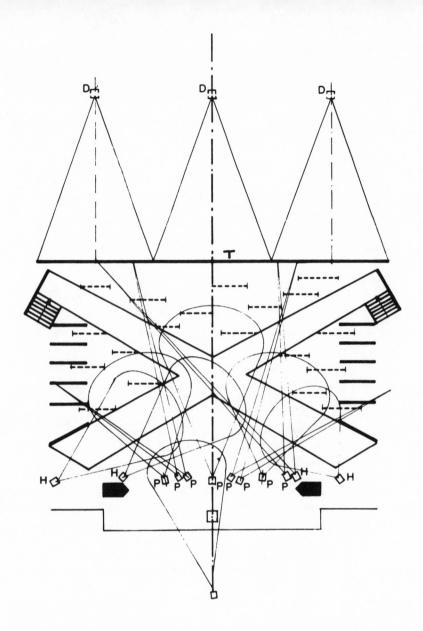

Figure 31. Ground plan of the Covent Garden *Tannhäuser*, act 3, but representative of the basic projection system for all three acts. The repeated short segments of broken lines indicate the suspended scrim panels that were lowered into the spaces between the crossed paths: *T*, cyclorama of Studio folio; *H*, Pani 5-kw. halogen projectors; *P*, Pani 2-kw. halogen projectors; *D*, Reiche Vogel 3-kw. projectors.

placed among clusters of small projection surfaces, and Scriabin's composition included systematic notations for colored lighting in *Prometheus*.)[3]

In the Covent Garden *Tannhäuser* Svoboda drew on these and earlier experiments. The basic approach was very similar to that of the Hamburg *Tannhäuser*: for the Venusberg, a combination of mirrors and projected images above raised paths that remained as a constant architectural unit for the entire production; here, however, the paths took the form of a cross (fig. 31). The second scene was virtually the same as that in Hamburg: a series of scrim panels lowered into pockets formed by the crossed paths and onto which foliage was projected. The third scene varied somewhat from its prototype in Hamburg. For the Wartburg scene Svoboda changed from a system of pure lighting and architecture to one of projections and architecture. The Romanesque cornice remained virtually the same, but instead of the contralighting that silhouetted it, Svoboda filled a folio cyclorama with a rear projection of a stained-glass window (fig. 32). At those points of the action when the Venus motif was present, the stained–glass image reversed from positive to negative, or supplementary, abstract, blood-red images were cast on the basic image of stained

glass. In the final scene in the valley, Tannhäuser's vision of Venus was created by a rear-projected slide image of Venus that could be seen on the cyclorama throughout the scrim panels.

Most of the striking variations, however, occurred in the first scene. The principal one was the use of *inflated* gray Studio folio to create rounded forms some nine feet high in the side and rear cavities formed by the cross (plates 2, 3). The inflation itself was a relatively quick, simple matter requiring only a small amount of air pressure from fans, and the deflated forms could be walked on. Why this pneumatic scenery? The rounded forms themselves suggested female anatomy. Moreover, they extended and amplified the use of projections and shadows. As in Hamburg, an array of projectors cast images on the outer surface of the inflated forms, but in Covent Garden these frontal projections were supplemented by eight projectors *within* the inflated forms, each with thirty or more slides, thus creating a multiple barrage of images on the inner surfaces of these translucent forms. Dancers within the inflated forms, casting their shadows on the inner surface, were to complete the effect.

Implicit in this system was a much more sophis-

Figure 32. Units of benches were moved into the spaces around the paths for act 2, the Wartburg scene, in both *Tannhäusers*. The only other tangible element was a silhouetted cornice. This photo of the Covent Garden production shows the rear-projected stained-glass window that was added. *Photograph by Group Three Photography, Ltd.*

ticated, complex, largely preprogrammed cuing system. Cues were marked on an annotated piano score held by one person in the control booth, who signaled the lighting crew. Some cues were preset for entire sequences.[4] The system created a greater variety of shifting images than had been possible in Hamburg, including a broader range of emotional overtones suggested by the colors that changed from warm to cool during the scene and ended with a dull gray as the forms deflated in the transition to the next scene. The projected images also changed, from sexually suggestive abstract textures and forms to spectral colors hand-painted on glass slides and microphotographs of crystals and minerals. The sensual element was further reduced at Covent Garden by shaping the mirrors in more abstract, free-form patterns, almost like leaves, rather than in curves suggesting female anatomy.

One of the many problems that plagued this production grew from the abandonment of the original idea of having dancers within the inflated forms casting erotically suggestive shadows on the forms. The practical problem of keeping the folios inflated while allowing small openings at floor level through which the dancers could enter or exit was easily solved, for the escaping air was not sufficient to affect the inflated forms. An *artistic* decision by some of the Covent Garden staff, however, placed the dancers, not inside the inflated forms, but outside on the crossed paths, thereby diminishing part of the intended visual effect. The kind of dancing finally selected, as well as the difficulties of blocking the movement of the chorus on the crossed paths in subsequent scenes, created other problems. The projections themselves, in both the Venusberg and valley sequences, came in for their share of criticism as being too garish, or faded, or simply too numerous.[5] But the total scenography found its defenders among the critics. Some applauded the successful ambivalence created by the scenography;[6] Max Loppert hailed the special "hallucinatory, 'trip' manner not entirely untrue to the spirit of the music. . . . it has a definite visual flavor."[7] On the whole, however, the production did not elicit a reception comparable to the amount of imagination and ingenuity that went into the scenography. Nevertheless, Svoboda had added to the range of scenographic systems and had produced still another variation in his creation of what he calls psychoplastic space, space that is expressively alterable in response to the dramatic action or musical score.

Chapter 5   *Tristan und Isolde*

Tristan und Isolde was written in the late 1850s, when Wagner was in the midst of working on the much vaster canvas of the *Ring* and most strongly under the influence of Arthur Schopenhauer. The most lyrical and subjective of Wagner's operas, it deals with the forbidden and ultimately fatal love between Isolde and Tristan, an overwhelming passion that sweeps aside all rational codes and welcomes death as the culmination of their ecstatic union. Wagner's own remarks make clear the special focus of the piece: "Life and death, the whole import and existence of the outer world, here hangs on nothing but the inner movements of the soul."[1] With its rejection of outer reality, and ultimately of life itself, and its withdrawal into a state of rapture composed of the spiritual and the erotic, the opera came to be viewed as a definitive example of late romantic decadence. It also served as an inspiration for Baudelaire, Mallarmé, and the entire symbolist movement. In his lengthy analysis of the opera, Adolphe Appia concentrated, as Wagner did, on the crucial significance of the inner action; he proposed that a staging of the opera should make the audience perceive the drama through the eyes of the central figures, thus suggesting a virtually expressionistic approach.[2] The problem in staging *Tristan*, however,

is the constant *duality* of an outer and inner reality, the harsh world and the transcendent spirit. The staging needs to reflect both the external world and the passion-driven withdrawal of the soul toward darkness, night, and death.

Svoboda feels that *Tristan* is probably the most beautiful Wagner opera and more challenging than even the *Ring*. He has designed *Tristan* three times. The first production, directed by Claus Helmut Drese, occurred at Wiesbaden in 1967 and was repeated with slight modifications at Cologne a few months later. The second production was in 1974 at Bayreuth itself, the home of the prototypal productions, the most recent of which had been Wieland Wagner's production in the early 1960s. Svoboda's was the first *Tristan* at Bayreuth in nearly thirty years not designed or directed by the Wagners. These first two *Tristans* had a number of scenographic elements in common, chiefly the use of projections on dense clusters of strung cords; although there were a number of interesting differences as well, the second production could be considered an evolution of the first. The third production, at Geneva in 1978, was a notable departure in that it was based on an all-encompassing architectural principle supplemented by

special lighting and projection effects. Svoboda was particularly pleased by the purity and rightness of his scenographic solution for his third *Tristan*.

THE WIESBADEN-COLOGNE PRODUCTIONS

The Wiesbaden-Cologne productions of 1967 brought together three scenographic elements: a symbolic, metaphoric construction, a new form of cyclorama, and specialized lighting effects. The symbolic construction element was a large, downward spiral that dominated the center of the stage (figs. 33–35) and was intended by Svoboda to stress the fated culmination of the action: "The whole opera is marked by its end — there is no solution except death, it's inevitable. And the spiral embodies this. It creates a meeting point and a point of no escape."

The second element formed the central scenographic principle of the production: a system of strung cords that created a dispersed, spatial cyclorama intended to provide greater dimension and texture to the lighting and incidental projections. Svoboda had used cords or thin strips before, but he recalls this as his first use of cords as a fundamental, general feature for an entire

production. The cords combined with infinitely variable colored lighting to suggest the shifting states of mind and soul of the central characters. A certain moiré effect, created by the slightly varying slant of the cords, added to the subjective, emotive quality of the staging. Moreover, the cords were able to take projections, which in this production were limited to abstract images of sails to suggest the shipboard locale of the first act. Otherwise, only colored light was used in the remaining acts.

Svoboda employed, although sparingly, a highly dramatic lighting effect in the climactic moments of the first and third acts. An intangible column of light enclosed the lovers to convey the burning intensity of their passion. Its method of operation is characteristic of Svoboda's creative use of technology. A series of low-voltage units was placed around the center of the spiral, aimed directly upward. Ten or fifteen minutes before the column or pillar of light was to materialize, an aerosol spray of droplets was released above the lights to create a dense atmosphere that would remain invisible until the desired moment. Only when the lights were brought up to full intensity did the glowing, burning column materialize as an impalpable substance created

Figure 34. In the Cologne variant of *Tristan*, a folio cyclorama facilitated a combination of rear and frontal projection.

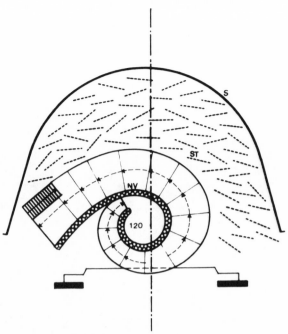

Figure 35. Ground plan of 1967 Cologne production: *NV*, low-voltage lighting units positioned at stage level; *ST*, cotton cords, gray (only an approximate indication); *S*, curved cyclorama of Studio folio.

by light. A basic problem had to be solved, however, before this effect was achieved. The droplets evaporated quickly in the heat of the lights or clustered together forming a cloud or smoke effect rather than an evenly distributed mass. Adding oil to the water retarded evaporation, but not until a positive electrical charge was added to the droplets by means of an electrostatic filter did the droplets repel each other and thereby stay suspended in the desired consistency and distribution.

A few other refinements are worth noting. Maintaining the tautness of the cords was a problem at Wiesbaden; the tautness was achieved at Cologne by attaching a rubber band to one end of each cord. Wiesbaden backed up the cords with black velour. Cologne used Studio folio, a change that made possible a sparing use of rear-projected cloudlike abstract images to reinforce the frontal lighting and sail projections.

The Wiesbaden-Cologne *Tristan* was a pioneering venture in the use of strung cords and special lighting in conjunction with an architectonic construction. In retrospect, however, Svoboda believed that the effect of the cords was too smooth and flat, and that the use of projections on the cords was not fully exploited. Moreover, the dimension and placement of the cords might

have been improved. In the Wiesbaden-Cologne *Tristan* the cords were approximately five millimeters in diameter, and spaced five centimeters apart. They were arranged in sections about four to six cords deep and a meter wide with the sections separated by varying distances up to one meter. For a number of reasons, Svoboda looked forward to using this particular scenographic system again and developing its possibilities. The opportunity came in the Bayreuth production of *Tristan* in 1974.

THE BAYREUTH PRODUCTION

The scenography of the Bayreuth *Tristan*[3] loaded the projections-on-cord system with maximum significance as a visual embodiment of the inner passions of the music drama, while cutting down on the symbolic values of the tangible, constructed elements of the set. The aim, said Svoboda, was to create a color-drenched *atmosphere* for each scene, not a concretely represented place. Svoboda's original plan (later modified) called for the extensive use of wholly abstract, pointillistic slides to be projected onto the cords. The slides would provide a deeply textured effect and create projected images that

Figure 36. Act 1 of the Bayreuth *Tristan* in 1974, showing the basic ground plan and the sail of perforated Studio folio (a folio variant also used later in the Covent Garden *Rheingold*). Subsequently, a sail of heavy scrim was substituted for the folio.

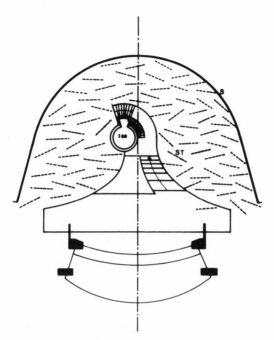

Figure 37. Ground plan for act 2 of the Bayreuth *Tristan*: S, cyclorama of Studio folio; *ST*, cords of gray cotton, reinforced with nylon.

were atomized, very much like painting in space or, as Svoboda suggested, like a transition to holography. A corollary of this was a complex, richly orchestrated system of changes in the color and form of the lighting and projections; the changes were to reflect the changing emotional states with great precision and thus induce the audience to "enter into the score." The standard projection instruments were supplemented by six Pani 4-Kw. BP4 HMI (halogen metal vapor) units, the most powerful available at the time. The array of projectors was aimed at the strings from both the front and sides and, for the second, nocturnal act, from high in the rear in a contralighting position casting images through the cords onto the stage floor. The intention was to create psychoplastic space by means of projections on cords.

A denser arrangement of thinner cords was another contributing detail in the Bayreuth production. The absolutely vertical cords, 2.5 millimeters in diameter and 2.5 centimeters apart, were arranged in sections six to eight rows deep around three sides of a basic unit set, consisting of convex sides leading to a flight of stairs upstage center. With minor adjustments this grouping of elements functioned as the ship, the tower and forest, and the rampart of a castle at the edge of the sea (figs.

36, 37). The Bayreuth production established a more humanized, realistic world; the Wiesbaden-Cologne production, by contrast, with its austere spiral, left more to the imagination of the spectator. The quality of relative realism at Bayreuth was enhanced by a large chorus, a sail in act 1, and a tree in act 3, as well as by the use of a Studio folio cyclorama backing up the cords. Although there were no rear projections on this folio, the folio cyclorama created a naturalistic sky effect.

August Everding, the director, stressed the break in each act between what he called "reality and transcendency," achieved by the combination of general lighting and projections. In act 1, for example, a strange, eclipse-like effect of darkness at noon occurred after Tristan and Isolde drank the potion. They were then isolated in a pool of the deepest blue light imaginable, illuminated by what appeared to be moonlight against the ghostly white sail behind them. In act 2, probably the most successful in creating the desired effect, a dappled, autumnal, shimmering light on the cords and floor established the real world (plate 4). Then the lighting faded to more abstract, muted colors and projected forms that blended into increasingly dark brown hues until the critical moment deep in the love scene. At this

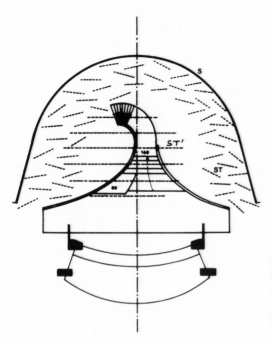

Figure 38. Ground plan of act 3: *S*, cyclorama of Studio folio; *ST*, cotton cords; *ST'*, special sections of cords weighted with metal tubes 15 cm. long and of the same diameter as the cords, which were crimped within the tubes. *Tristan*, Bayreuth, 1974.

point, a midnight blue was injected into the total picture, evolving toward a virtual blackout with occasional subtle shifts of abstract projected images.

The treatment of act 3 merits special attention. The trunk of a tree was created by casting the shadow of a special flat onto the rear of the folio cyclorama, and the crown of the tree by suspending at irregular heights above the stage a large cluster of shorter cords with metallic ends approximately fifteen centimeters long (plate 5, figs. 38–39). This mass of cords was illuminated by projectors containing the pointillistic slides—in this case, the patterns projected were painted directly on the glass of the slides for added intensity. All of the projectors carried transparencies eighteen by eighteen centimeters (seven by seven inches), which make for larger and more intense images than one normally obtains from carousel slide projectors. The two different kinds of images projected, respectively, on two different kinds of cord projection surfaces created an especially strong visual impression. But the climactic transformation occurred at the end of the act, capturing the transcendent *Liebestod* in visual terms. At the decisive moment, a series of halogen flood lamps hidden behind the walls and aimed directly upward at the special cords were turned on. Simultaneously, the pointillistic slides were removed from the four projectors aimed at the special cords forming the crown of the tree, leaving the intense light from the halogen projectors with no interference save a light blue filter. Finally four additional projectors with no slides were added to the crown, thus creating an overwhelming, dazzling cloud of light in contrast to the darkness that enveloped Tristan and Isolde.

The production verified for Svoboda the efficacy of the strung cord system as a new form of cyclorama in depth, one that has no folds, can be walked through, can virtually disappear depending on the lighting, and takes projections to create a feeling of three-dimensional colored light. Svoboda's production was also the occasion for a number of compromises and sacrifices between the original conception and the final result on stage; some of these changes are worth noting as examples of the problems of actual production, when technical limitations and differences of artistic opinion make themselves felt.

Svoboda originally planned an even more abstract, less realistic production. For example, hundreds of the pointillistic, abstract slides that were to form the basis of all the lighting effects were scrapped; only the special slides

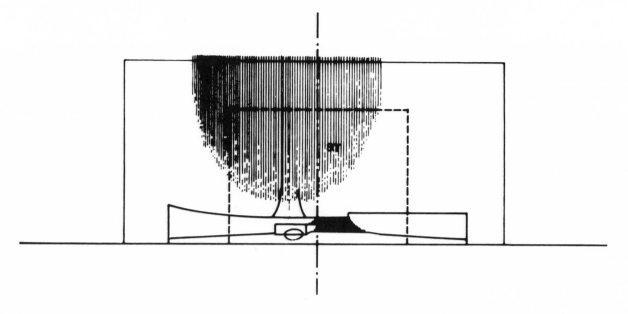

Figure 39. Frontal elevation of act 3, isolating the special cords that formed the crown of the tree.

Figure 40. Svoboda's model for his original plan for the tree in act 3 of the Bayreuth *Tristan:* a three-dimensional trunk and a grouping of specially sprayed, crumpled wire screening for the crown.

used for the night scene of act 2 and the crown in act 3 were retained. Photographs of real subjects (leaves, clouds, and so on), distanced from a naturalistic norm by being slightly out of focus, enlarged, or otherwise slightly distorted, were substituted for the pointillistic patterns. The final visual effects were in any case impressive; one can only speculate what they would have been if the original concept had been used in all three acts.

The sail that appeared in act 1 was a third scenographic choice. Originally there was to be no sail, only a small folding screen to demarcate Isolde's chamber. The screen was eliminated in rehearsals, and a sail of Studio folio (which responded to counterlighting by taking on a luminous, nearly white hue) was substituted. Finally, a sail of heavier-than-usual scrim took the place of the folio sail because the latter would tear under the stress of being pulled back and forth. Svoboda, however, was not able to regard either of the sails as an organic part of the setting.

Other interesting changes occurred in the third act. Although the original scheme included a three-dimensional, central tree, exigencies of blocking made the final trunk a two-dimensional shadow. For Svoboda,

however, the graphic quality seemed inconsistent with the basically three-dimensional nature of the strung cord system. Moreover, the crown of the tree was originally to have been formed of clusters of crumpled wire screening sprayed with paint around the edges so as to create a mass with no clearly defined edges (fig. 40). The screening would have been barely visible until illuminated by projections. At the culminating moment of transformation and transcendence, according to the original concept, Tristan and Isolde would have been elevated on a lift thrusting from under a Lastex ground cloth. At the same time, the crumpled screening would have been lowered, and its projection transformed from tree crown to clouds, while the basic cord system would have turned to the dark blue of the stratosphere. The total effect would have been that of Tristan and Isolde experiencing a transcendence of time and space. The cords with metal ends substituted for the original screening, the metal ends having the primary purpose of providing weight to facilitate the lowering of the strings. Finally, of course, the whole kinetic effect was deleted, but the metallic ends of the cords remained to intensify the revised moment of transcendence.

After the frustrations of the Bayreuth *Tristan* pro-

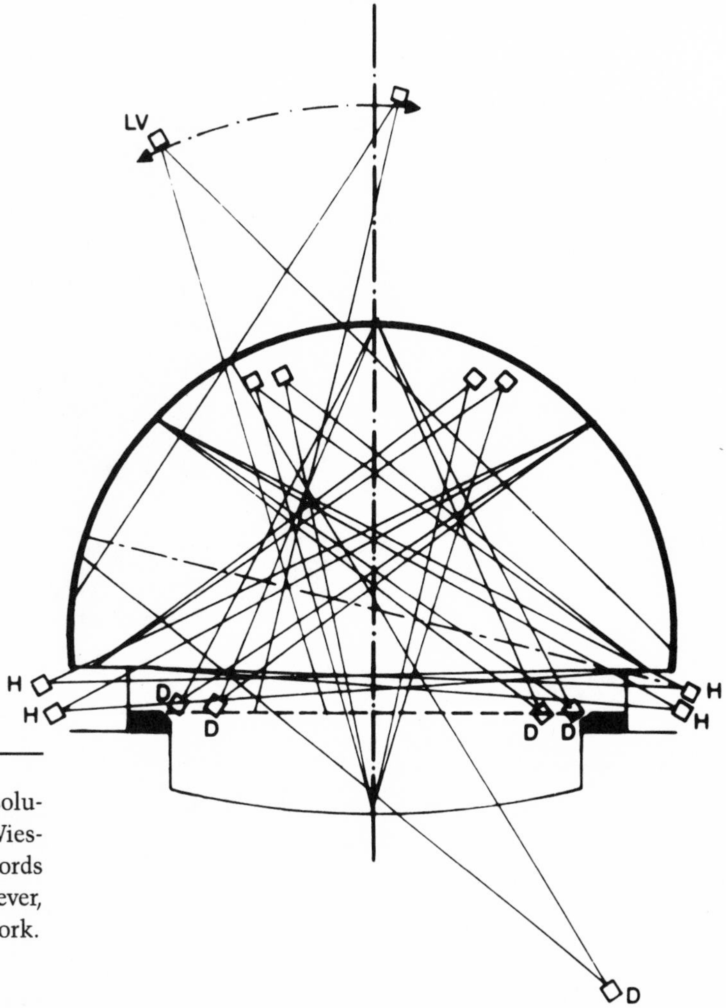

Figure 41. Basic ground plan and positioning of main lighting units for the *Tristan* at Geneva in 1978: *H*, Pani 4-kw. HMI projectors, 18-by-18-cm. format; *D*, Pani 5-kw. halogen projectors, 18-by-18-cm. format; *LV*, one section of ADB low-voltage lighting units that could "travel" during the course of the action (see figs. 45a, b); the unmarked small squares represent Reiche Vogel 1,000-watt low-voltage spotlights.

duction, Svoboda felt that an ideal scenographic solution for the opera would be a combination of the Wiesbaden-Cologne spiral with the Bayreuth system of cords *and the pointillistic slides.* A few years later, however, he tried still another system for the staging of this work.

THE GENEVA PRODUCTION

Svoboda's most recent production of *Tristan* returned to the architectonic principle of a significant material construction as the primary scenographic element, in this case a remarkable three-dimensional ellipsoid that enclosed and formed the total stage space, thereby functioning as acting area and cyclorama in one (fig. 41). Only in a theater like Geneva's, which produces operas serially, was this contruction possible. An alternating repertory system would have demanded the repeated and unfeasible erection and striking of the ellipsoid. The intention of the ellipsoid was to create what Svoboda called "absolute space," although the form could perhaps also be associated with a nucleus or womb, a visual impression that echoed the basic form used by Svoboda in his design of the *Ring* at Geneva several years earlier (see chapter 6). Of special significance are the purity of

Figure 42. Act 2 of the Geneva *Tristan*. The tower has been reduced to a balcony downstage left.

the design and the extremely abstract, spatial nature of this approach, which was reinforced by the omission of all but the most essential details; for example, the tower usually represented in act 2 was reduced to a small balcony in the downstage-left proscenium arch (figs. 42, 43). Similarly, color was largely absent; a subdued atmosphere prevailed, with occasional use of color for dramatic accent.

The one supplementary scenographic element consisted of projections, and once again, initial concept differed from final result. Svoboda originally conceived the idea of a triptych of projections, including some on film, to accompany the action on the principle of follow spots. At key moments, both Tristan and Isolde would have been followed by a projector in which each slide or film frame had a blank center; this would have produced the combined effect of a follow spot and a distinct, symbolically apt background or "world" for each character during a crucial emotional peak. The result might be the juxtaposition of abstract images suggesting storm, landscape, waves, flame, and so on. The third projector of the triptych would have provided a generalized background for those moments as well as others. Amid the realities of rehearsal schedules and pressures,

Figure 43. Another set of projections for act 2 of *Tristan* at Geneva, 1978.

Figure 44. Act 1 of the Geneva *Tristan*, indicating the disposition of the two stylized sails.

however, the triptych principle was abandoned, and what remained was the one projector for general background elements, such as clouds or the tree.

In the Geneva production, the sails in act 1 were part of Svoboda's original planning (plate 6, fig. 44). The one sail of the Bayreuth production became two sails in Geneva, both of scrim: a small sail on a mast in front of a larger sail close to the wall of the ellipsoid. The small one could be lowered completely to the floor. Another interesting effect was a bank of low-voltage spotlights in a contralight position behind the ellipsoid and shining through its arched opening in act 3. Functioning as the sun, the unit moved along a suspended track, casting its beams and creating shadows along a path on the stage floor and finally catching the prone Tristan in its rays (plate 7, figs. 45a,b).

Considered together, the three *Tristans* reveal a number of Svoboda's specific techniques and several underlying characteristics of his creative approach. Svoboda's scenes reflect a preference for abstract, functional forms though not to the exclusion of realistic associations. Moreover, he is consistently interested in the fundamental prob-

lems of shaping a stage space. Svoboda has both the urge and the expertise to continue experimenting with a variety of methods and devices in order to evolve scenographic systems that are of the theater rather than those that merely borrow from other artistic disciplines to provide background decor. These fundamental characteristics were, if anything, even more evident in his work on two productions of Wagner's *Ring des Nibelungen*, the massive tetralogy that has understandably been regarded as the Everest of operas. The two *Rings* (London and Geneva) were produced between the second and third *Tristans*. Although certain echoes and variations among these several productions will be apparent, it would be difficult to perceive any routine carryover among these works. Each bears distinctive features.

Plate 6.
Tristan, act 1 (Geneva 1978)

Plate 7.
Tristan, act 3 (Geneva 1978)

Plate 8.
Laser projection

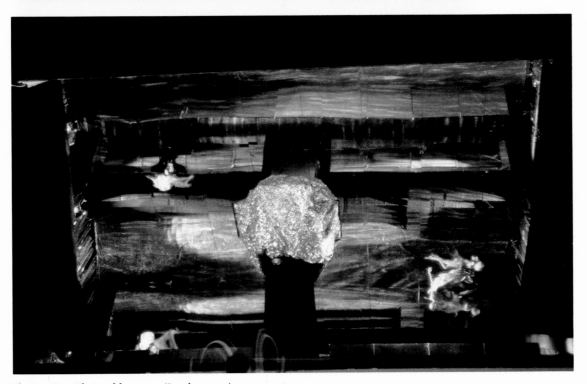

Plate 9. *Das Rheingold*, scene 1 (London 1974)

Plate 10.
Die Walküre, act 3
(London 1974)

Plate 11.
Siegfried, act 1
(London 1975)

Plate 12.
Götterdämmerung, act 1,
scene 1 (London 1976)

Plate 13. *Das Rheingold,* scene 4 (Geneva 1975)

Figure 47. One of the many positions assumed by the Covent Garden platform. *Photograph by Group Three Photography, Ltd.*

of the orchestra suggests tragedy. A rectangular platform (a mime stage!) aids that which is epic and tends toward comedy . . . *comedie humaine!*"[4] The platform is a lattice-framed construction measuring approximately thirty-seven by thirty-two feet, two feet thick. Its undersurface is mirrored and its top capable of varied treatment. The decisive feature of the platform, however, is its mobility. It can sink more than six feet below stage level or rise more than ten feet above it; it can tilt up to forty-five degrees in any direction, and it can rotate. Supporting the platform is a three-section telescoping tower with two large lifting rams; all movements are hydraulically and remotely controlled by hand-held units using electroproportional servo-control valves.[5] Most remarkable of all is that the movements of the platform are silent.

The platform, the single unifying element of the total production, also allows for the wide range of effects Friedrich and Svoboda require. It can be a static area virtually indistinguishable from the regular stage level at Covent Garden; it can interact kinetically with the performers and the music; it can become one or several staircases; it can function as a giant mirror reflecting action beneath the level of the stage; it can become a surface for projections. In its specific functions and dramatic versatility it recalls special scenographic constructions in such Svoboda works as Shakespeare's *Romeo and Juliet* (Prague, 1963), Bertolt Brecht's *Mother Courage* (Prague, 1970), and the never-produced version of Sergei Prokofiev's *Fiery Angel* (Milan, 1970). A unique scenographic *instrument* helping to express a multitude of dramatic states, it contains great metaphoric power by virtue of its very existence as a stage within a stage, a platform stage as basic and simple as those found throughout theater history, yet charged with a special reality. Svoboda has elaborated on these points:

We didn't want it to be a ring or anything circular, but a stage. And we think and believe that we gave ourselves an absolute freedom, and an instrument that is capable of interpreting everything that we need. . . . Can we have a nineteenth-century stage dragon and laser beams? The answer is yes if we're playing theater—world theater. We have the right because the moment that we elected to have an ordinary stage, a platform, a stage floor, we created the right to play theater from antiquity onward, perhaps even Chinese theater. Because we are doing theater of completely different kinds, four works, a *commedia divina*. Why not confront it with all the means at our disposal?

Of course they will have the same signature in terms of one director and one designer, but why not learn from the whole history of theater, and why not use anything and everything that expresses it 100 percent at the right moment, in the right way?

Supplementing the platform were a variey of scenographic elements that can best be described in relation to the staging of each opera. But one constant supplement, laser projections, should be mentioned first. A laser (the term is an acronym for light amplification by stimulated emission of radiation) is a device that produces a narrow, intense beam of coherent light—that is, light waves of a single frequency, in phase, and traveling in the same direction. The laser beam has had many scientific and technical applications, but few besides Svoboda have used it in scenography.[6] In both of his *Ring* productions, laser beams were used to create moving patterns of light projected onto cycloramas or even parts of the set as an abstract, expressive accompaniment to the music and action, primarily in introductory or transitional passages (plate 8). The projections were actually created by passing the original red, blue, or green laser beams through special glass filters that refracted the beams in patterns determined by the granular structure of the glass and its movement.

Svoboda and Friedrich created the sequence of patterns while listening to a recording of the operas in Erlangen, Germany, where the Siemens equipment and laboratory are located. These dynamic patterns were rear-projected onto a dark folio and filmed from the front on sixteen-millimeter film, which was then projected during the performance. In other words, in the Covent Garden *Ring* production, the laser projections were determined with considerable precision and fixed. The intention, it should be stressed, was to produce not a tight correspondence between the images and the musical score but rather an impressionistic accompaniment. In the performances, the laser projections played a dominant visual role only now and then; for the most part they were one element in the total lighting plan and never distracting.

One might ask, Why use laser projections at all? Why not some other source of intense light? The answer is that laser projections are more intense or vivid than most other comparable projections, and they are more readily programmable. Svoboda said that achieving a comparable effect by producing and filming a carbon arc beam, for example, would be much more unwieldy and expensive.

Das Rheingold

At the very beginning of *Das Rheingold* occurred a striking example of the employment of the laser projections and the platform. The platform lay dimly lit slightly above stage level, square to the audience, with its upstage edge slightly tilted up, like a neutral, vaguely perceived, enigmatic piece of the stage. The houselights went out and, as the prelude began, a spark of red light was cast onto the dark cyclorama: the inception of life. The spark became a streak, then a swirl of ever-changing red and blue patterns as the platform silently rose, leveled, and began to rotate slowly. Out of the void, creation and matter. Svoboda described the event: "We have created a world. Our world. The world of the *Ring*. We've given birth to a stage, bare boards, the plainest stage floor, the most simple reality."

When the platform's rotation stopped, its front edge tilted up to reveal the Rhine and its maidens, reflected from their position in the trap area beneath stage level by the mirrored undersurface of the platform, very much like the effect in the Hamburg *Tannhäuser*. The central support of the platform was covered with crumpled Mylar and spotlighted with gold light to represent a huge nugget: the gold of the Rhine (plate 9). Laser projections bridged the scene changes, along with the rotation and tilting of the platform. For the second scene, in the mountains, the action occurred on the smooth top surface of the platform, now moderately raked toward the audience (fig. 48). In the background, behind a cyclorama of light gray, *perforated* Studio folio, one could dimly perceive angular forms, while frontal cloud projections scudded across the face of the cyclorama. The angular forms represented Valhalla, but their actual construction became apparent only later, in the final scene. In the meantime, the next scene occurred below the earth's (or stage's) surface, in the subterranean realm of the Nibelungs, where scurrying, dwarfish miners were dominated by Alberich from his futuristic command module, a squat turret built of many magnifying lenses that grotesquely enlarged his features. Once again, most of the action was mirrored by the undersurface of the platform. Especially striking was the

Figure 48. Scene 2 of *Das Rheingold* at Covent Garden, 1974. The platform is virtually level, though slightly raised above stage level. Valhalla is dimly perceived behind the perforated Studio folio. The V-shaped image is caused by reflections of light from the Valhalla mirrors striking the rear of the translucent folio. (The spacesuit costuming of the two giants was not a motif carried through in the other operas; a deliberate eclecticism prevailed.) *Photograph by Group Three Photography, Ltd.*

vision of massive, glowing ingots being hammered and tempered; these were actually rectangular blocks with self-illuminated ends that were moved horizontally on the substage floor but appeared to be moving vertically in the mirrors (figs. 49, 50).

The final scene was again on top of the platform, now more sharply raked and revealing its power-operated flights of stairs, which unfolded automatically as soon as the platform reached an angle of twenty degrees from the horizontal. The stairs became the means for the gods' ascent to Valhalla, which was now completely revealed. At the god Donner's signal, the folio cyclorama sank down, and behind it one saw clearly the special construction of Valhalla, which moved forward several feet once the cyclorama had been lowered (figs. 51–53). As distinct from the platform, Valhalla consisted of a separate, smaller unit of fixed stairs located above and behind the main platform; on cue it was able to roll forward, joining the uptilted rear edge of the platform to form one extended flight of stairs. The vague angular forms on the Valhalla stairs were some twenty-five narrow rectangular mirrors of varying widths set irregularly at nine different stair levels, suggesting in highly abstract fashion a sense of impersonal, remote power.

The mirrored surfaces reflected interesting patterns of lights onto the rear of the folio when it was in position, and now, with the folio removed, the mirrors reflected the gods. Moreover, once the folio sank, the Valhalla stairs were seen to form a spectrum, the rainbow bridge itself, by means of lights placed behind the stair risers. Since the rears of the mirrors were also painted, those mirrors that reflected the backs of other mirrors revealed a cubistic extension of the spectrum. This effect is another echo of the Hamburg *Tannhäuser* system of mirrors.

According to Friedrich, the stark quality of the platform in *Das Rheingold* was intended to recall

the theater of the Mystery plays and early Soviet revolutionary plays: a theatricalized world order; a theater that provides the world with order. . . .The different regions are clearly separated: above are the giants and the gods, in the middle the Rhine, and below—living without treaties—the Nibelungens. . . . Long diagonals and strong slants signal the threat to this world order that originally seemed harmonized.[7]

Of central significance throughout the performance was Friedrich's skillful *use* of the platform in relation to the tableaux and movements of the actors, creating a total, orchestrated visual embodiment of Wagner's music

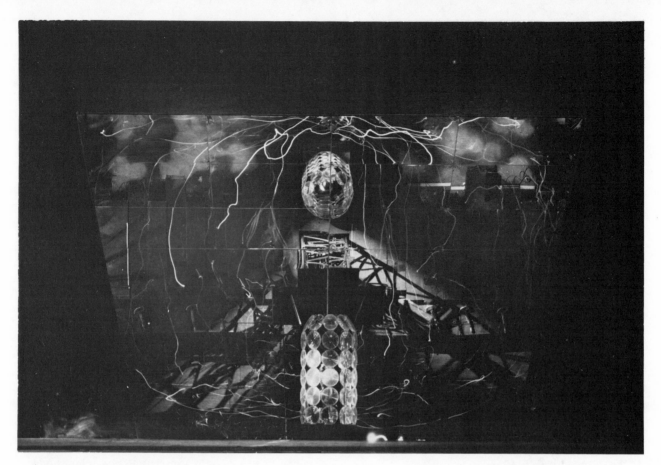

Figure 49. Scene 3 of *Das Rheingold*, the Nibelheim cavern. Alberich's module is at stage center. The mirrored undersurface of the platform reflects the top of the module as well as blurred streaks of the moving laborers in the trap area.

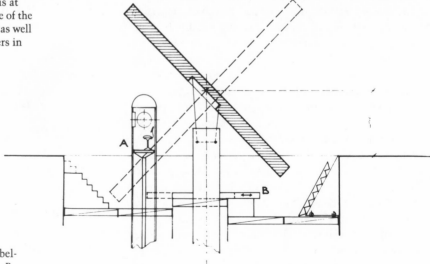

Figure 50. Side view of set for 1974 Nibelheim sequence: *A*, Alberich's module; *B*, the horizontally movable "ingots."

Figure 51. The final scene of *Das Rheingold* at Covent Garden presents the platform in a relatively steeply raked position. The five center sections of stairs have opened out automatically, leaving the two side sections in their flattened position. The Valhalla unit has moved forward and is much more visible because the cyclorama of Studio folio had by this time been lowered. Compare with figures 3 and 13. *Photograph by Group Three Photography, Ltd.*

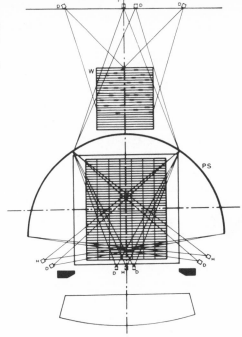

Figure 52. Ground plan and lighting positions for *Das Rheingold: PS*, perforated Studio folio; *H*, Pani 4-kw. HMI projectors, with 18-by-18-cm. transparencies; *D*, Pani 5-kw. halogen projectors; *W*, Valhalla; *F*, 16-mm. film projector, with 1,500-watt xenon lamp.

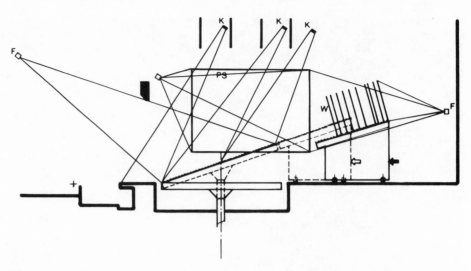

Figure 53. A side elevation that clarifies the movement of the Valhalla unit: *PS*, perforated Studio folio cyclorama, which was lowered to enable the Valhalla unit to move forward to join the main unit of stairs on the platform; *W*, Valhalla; *K*, contralights; *F*, 16-mm. film projection positions (the one in the auditorium was subsequently used to create an effect of fire in *Siegfried*).

drama in space and movement and light—not an illusion of reality but the shaping of a new reality that expresses Friedrich's and Svoboda's distinct vision or concept of Wagner's *Rheingold*.

Die Walküre

The same approach marked *Die Walküre* and the subsequent operas. For *Die Walküre*, the intention shifted toward a more traditionally pictorial stage of the nineteenth-century romantic, psychological drama, in order to depict what Friedrich called a "terminal epoch." The bare, austere platform was modified by adding a dark ground cloth and placing several abstract, monolithic forms on top of it, such as a massive tree trunk for the first scene in Hunding's home and two angled cliff formations for the subsequent scenes (figs. 54–56). These were supplemented by rock and cloud projections to heighten the sense of mountains in which the action occurs. The resulting variety of juxtaposed planes and acting areas, frequent changes in the platform's position, and expressive atmospheric lighting created a visually richer and more varied sequence of dynamic, restless compositions than occurred in *Das Rheingold*. The mirrored undersurface was used only once, to reflect the

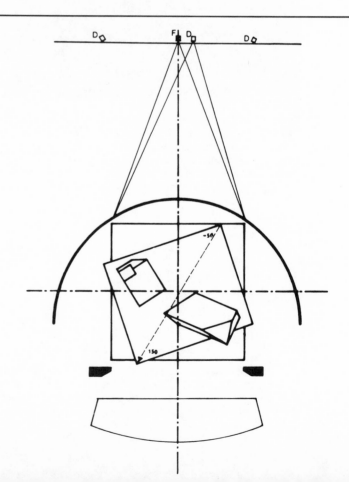

Figure 55. The first scene of *Die Walküre* at Covent Garden, showing the addition of a huge tree trunk to the platform.

Figure 54. The ground plan of the rocks on the platform: *D*, Pani 5-kw. halogen projectors; *F*, 16-mm. film projector.

Figure 56. Brünnhilde and Sieglinde in the mountains of act 2 of *Die Walküre*, Covent Garden, 1974.

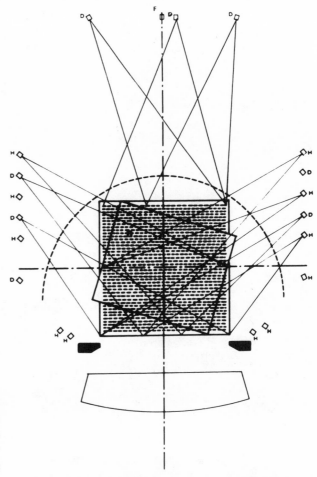

stormy scene of the Valkyries gathering slain heroes to bring to Valhalla (plate 10). A darker folio (Show folio) was used in this production, and the laser film was projected from the rear rather than the front, thereby creating more vivid images because the projector was closer to the projection surface. Moreover, rear projection itself—on this folio—creates more intense images than frontal projection.

Siegfried

Two noteworthy supplements to the platform were evident in *Siegfried*: a new top surface and an element suspended above the platform. To form the atmosphere of the forest scenes, Svoboda hung a dense array of strips of Studio folio, about six inches wide, arranged in some eight lateral rows above the platform stage and reaching down to lie on its surface. The strips were illuminated by green and yellow mottled projections and were in constant slight motion as a result of a flow of air from offstage fans (plate 11, fig. 57).

The other basic addition was a grillwork of "expanded metal" laid on top of the platform surface, forming a new surface of thin ridges enclosing small pockets about a quarter of an inch deep. The purpose was twofold: it

Figure 57. Ground plan of Covent Garden *Siegfried*, 1975, with lighting positions for the forest scenes: *H*, Pani 4-kw. HMI projectors; *D*, Pani 5-kw. projectors; hatching on the platform represents the strips of Studio folio.

Figure 58. The final scene of *Siegfried*, with the yet unawakened Brünnhilde on the single clifflike plinth now jutting out from the basic platform. Compare with figures 12 and 15.

Figure 59. Wotan's scene with Erda in act 3, scene 1, of the Covent Garden *Siegfried*. She is placed underneath him, as if part of the support of the column, and he as if an extension of it.

provided more secure footing for the performers on the tilted surface, but more important it facilitated both frontal projections onto the surface of the platform and contralighting from high upstage. Instead of the contralighting weakening any projected image on the floor, or even being reflected into the eyes of the audience, the frontally projected image would be more strongly reflected from the front of the vertical ridges, while the contralighting would be caught or deflected by the rear of the ridges. (Originally Svoboda had in mind much deeper ridges, forming channels more than an inch in depth and width, but their manufacture proved unfeasible at the time.) The dual effect of frontal projections with contralighting was most vital during act 3, scene 1, when Siegfried made his way through the fire surrounding Brünnhilde, which was actually a film of flames projected onto the surface of the platform. Accompanying this action was a deep tilting of the platform to reinforce the difficulty of Siegfried's challenge. When the platform finally stabilized in a forward-tilting position, still another new element was evident: a single plinth had emerged from the platform's surface, forming a stark cliff on which Brünnhilde lay (fig. 58). The resul-

tant tableau of spatial composition and evocative lighting formed one of the most impressive visual sequences of the entire *Ring*, recalling some of the strongest moments of the *Tristan* staging at Bayreuth, especially the isolation of the lovers in the second act.

A few other specific notes are worth adding. Two of Wagner's prime theatrical effects are the appearance of the dragon Fafner and of Erda, the earth mother. The platform itself and its support were employed effectively for the Erda sequence. The front edge of the platform was raised high, and while Wotan stood just behind the front edge, thus being raised in a central position, Erda was placed directly under him, as part of the supporting column, a caryatid, almost as if she herself were the support of the earth, an impression reinforced by rootlike filaments extending from her toward the platform. The total image was completed by Wotan's seeming to be an extension of Erda (fig. 59). The platform also played a role in the appearance of the dragon, first tilting back to allow the dragon to get onto the rear of the platform without being seen, and then tilting forward to reveal the monstrous creature in the thicket created by the suspended strips (fig. 60). In keeping with Friedrich's

Figure 60. Siegfried and the partially hidden, slain dragon in act 2 of *Siegfried* at Covent Garden. Each claw was manipulated by a youngster within it.

sense of *Siegfried* as, in part, a black comedy or "heroic comic strip," the dragon itself was a formidable, crablike beast, the torso of which resembled the turret of a tank (from which Fafner appeared), while each claw was large enough to contain a child who manipulated it (very likely the same children were used to swarm so frighteningly as the Nibelung dwarfs in *Das Rheingold*). The slain dragon was then removed by reversing the tilting process that brought it on.

A few problems may also be noted. In the original plan and actually in the first performances of this *Siegfried*, a cyclorama of strung black cords (on the *Tristan* principle) figured prominently, backing up the folio strips and enriching the various projections, but technical construction difficulties prevented its use when the entire *Ring* was presented on consecutive nights. Also, the folio strips themselves were not as effective as Svoboda wished them to be. He would have preferred an even denser accumulation, to heighten the sense of effort involved in characters struggling through them, but the director decided that visibility might become a problem.

The magic fire surrounding Brünnhilde was a chronic problem never fully solved, partly because fire regula-tions prevented the use of thin strips of fabric to represent flames. The various substitutes never quite produced the intensity and vividness that was sought; for example, the attempt to have two or more projectors casting images of flames onto the surface of the platform ironically produced a weaker impression of fire because the image from each projector weakened those of the others, on the principle of parasitic light weakening any projected image.

Götterdämmerung

Friedrich's vision of *Götterdämmerung*, in his program notes, was that of "the last station of the terminal action: the glittering glamour of the last civilization, a distorted image of the once heroic struggle to stave off downfall, encrusts everything like a living corpse, a future society without a future." Svoboda's scenographic image for this involved the addition of a series of glass and Plexiglas panels suspended above the platform in a number of vertical configurations for the Gibichung scenes, creating a dominant image of glittering coldness and suggesting something of today's banks, high-rise offices, or indeed George Orwell's *1984*. In design and imagery they also echoed the earlier mirror panels of

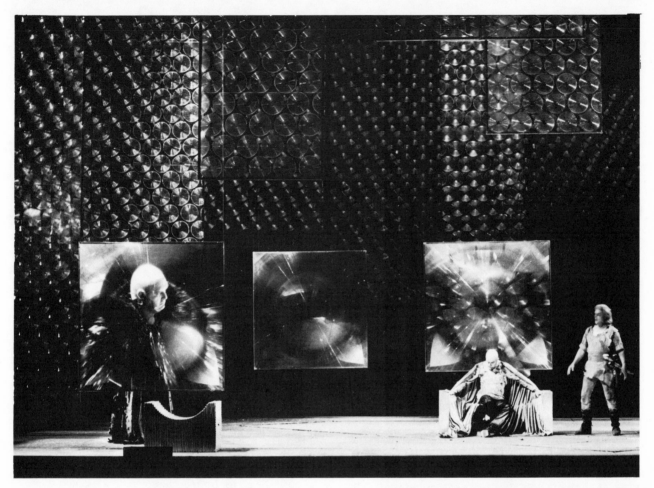

Figure 61. The three large magnifying lenses could provide an instant close-up effect. A particularly effective usage involved the enlarged image of the malicious Hagen eavesdropping on the others. Act 1, scene 1, *Götterdämmerung*, Covent Garden, 1976.

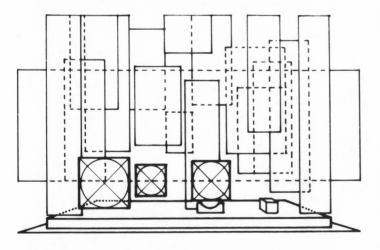

Figure 62. A schematic frontal view of the Gibichung Hall in the Covent Garden *Götterdämmerung* provides an overall perspective on the several elements of panels and magnifying lenses.

Valhalla (plate 12, fig. 62). Originally the panels were to have been plain glass or Plexiglas, but they evolved into a combination of several huge magnifying lenses and other panels studded with what were to be reducing lenses, which would create an image of hundreds of tiny scenes. Actually, only a few of the small lenses were reductive; the rest were simply plastic copies because the authentic ones could not be ordered in time. Although the huge magnifying lenses arrived too late to be integrated completely into the blocking, they added a number of dramatic moments, such as when Hagen's features were monstrously enlarged as he spied upon the actions of others, another striking echo of an earlier scene of Alberich, Hagen's father, in his command module in Nibelheim, in *Das Rheingold*.

Several scenes take place in the mountains where Siegfried and Brünnhilde meet, and the contrast between the austere and pure platform setting for these scenes and that for the Gibichung scenes was indeed striking, even though both scenes maintained a unity of design style. The scene of Siegfried's murder in the forest was equally austere: three huge, bare columns representing tree trunks marked the borders of the spot where Sieg-

Figure 63. The stark scene of the murder of Siegfried in act 3, scene 1, of the Covent Garden *Götterdämmerung*. The radically stylized columns representing trees suggest a nature that is ossified or from which all vitality has been removed.

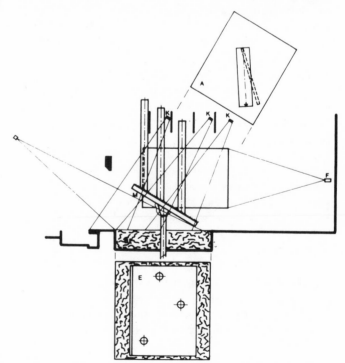

Figure 64. A side view depicts some of *Götterdämmerung's* other key settings at Covent Garden: *A*, a projected view of the platform surface with the protrudable Brünnhilde rock; *E*, a projected view of the arrangement of columns for the scene of Siegfried and the Rhine maidens as well as the scene of Siegfried's murder; *M*, mirrored surface; *K*, contralights; *F*, 16-mm. film projector. The squiggly lines in the trap area represent crumpled black plastic that was intended to give the effect of a polluted Rhine River.

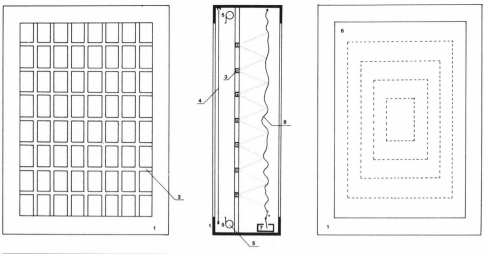

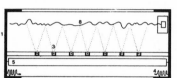

Figure 65. The funeral-pyre instrument for the end of the Covent Garden *Götter-dämmerung*: (1) The frame measured 300 by 400 by 100 cm. and was covered with black velour; (2) the gridwork consisted of welded steel U–channels, 30 by 30 mm., with 250-watt halogen lamps laid in the channels—112 lamps were used, for a total of 28 kw.; (3) halogen lamps; (4) vertical black velour shutter curtain; (5) horizontal black velour shutter curtain; (6) shutter curtains, with dotted lines indicating their operation; (7) vibrating motor that shakes the mirrored folio (8) to create a more vivid effect of fire.

fried is treacherously slain (figs. 63, 64). During the famous Funeral March music after his death, when stage curtains are usually closed until the next scene, the curtains remained open, with only a dim light around Siegfried's isolated body. The columns were lifted out in the prevailing darkness, and then the Gibichung panels were slowly lowered in, masking Siegfried's body in the process. As Hagen and others entered, the lights came up and the panels lifted slightly, revealing Siegfried's body as last seen: the body had been "transported" without ever being moved, a piece of staging that was typical of this production (the curtains never closed during scene changes). Most other changes were bridged by laser projections and movements of the platform.

Two spectacular events at the end of *Götterdämmerung* are the funeral pyre that consumes Siegfried and Brünnhilde and the fire that consumes Valhalla itself. The funeral pyre was one of the most powerful effects of the opera: an immense burst of flashes and flames, followed by smoke (fig. 65). The device that produced this effect consisted of a large square gridwork, the crosspieces of which were wide enough to contain powerful lights masked from the audience. The lights were aimed at the rear wall of this construction, which was covered with crumpled mirror foil that could be shaken to create a dazzling reflection straight out toward the audience. The sheer intensity of the concentrated, reflected light was strong enough to wipe out the visual impression of the crosspieces; all one saw was a mass of light and smoke feeding into the light from below stage. Amplifying the effect of fire were swirling red laser patterns and a projection of flames above the fiery construction itself. This effect dominated the burning fall of the Gibichung palace, which was produced by the rapid and irregular up-and-down movement of the glass panels, which were finally lifted out. All this action was supplemented by a projection resembling a vertically rising flow of red lava.

The burning of Valhalla itself was another scenographic coup. Two superimposed projections produced first an image of the Valhalla steps and mirrors as if covered by flame and then an image of the gods themselves seemingly sitting in the flames of Valhalla (figs. 66, 67). The first projection was film of a model of Valhalla, with a low fire in front of the model and the Valhalla mirrors reflecting another fire that was actually located behind the camera taking the picture. On top of this image was projected, during the actual

Figure 66. The drawing shows how the film of Valhalla in flames was made: (1) model of Valhalla; (2) low fire in front of the camera; (3) camera; (4) high fire behind the camera was reflected in the Valhalla mirrors.

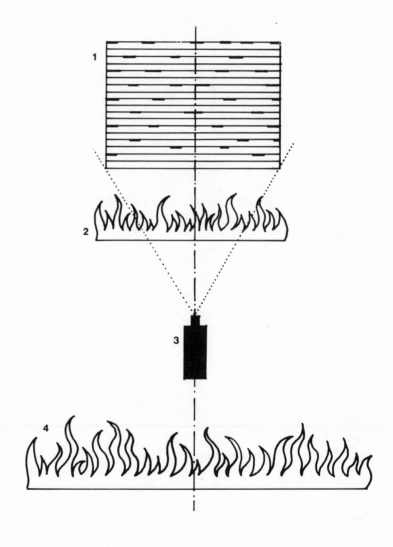

Figure 67. The burning of Valhalla was extremely hard to photograph adequately, but this shot may at least suggest the combination of projections that was involved.

performance, a slide image of the seated gods. This particular method was intended to achieve more control of the projection process and also to gain a more intense total image. Actually, in the performance I witnessed, this Valhalla effect seemed somewhat dim and diffuse, perhaps for the same reason that the magic fire around Brünnhilde seemed rather weak: two overlapping projected images are likely to be less vivid than one.

The other final effects of this opera consisted of the fall of Hagen into the Rhine (a fall from the front, uptilted edge of the platform into the trap area below the stage); the sporting of the Rhine maidens with their restored gold (on top of the platform, which by this time had reversed its tilt and had a flowing water projection on its surface); and the final visual moment of the platform returned to its original, almost level position in the dim light, with only a few remaining traces of smoke. Once again we were confronted with a bare, neutral form: the eternal stage. Götz Friedrich felt it could be read as an invitation to play the *Ring* once more: "a different *Ring*, with different people and new experiences. . . . Every ending conceals a new beginning, and only that could mean a step forward toward Utopia."[8]

There is no surer way of destroying the total impression of a work than by describing its individual details. In attempting to recapture the essential overall impression of this production of the *Ring*, one must return to the platform itself, the central image and instrument that provided unity and dynamics, that implicitly conveyed the sense of *theater* so crucial for both Friedrich and Svoboda. For Svoboda it became a "classic, almost universal intrument," significant for its symbolic value but even more for its functional, "play" values, its becoming part of the action. "To me, a scenographer with over four hundred productions, the platform seems a miracle. I wouldn't dare ask for anything better, because a platform that moves in any way I want it to move, and silently, is a supreme stage reality, a stage miracle." Svoboda's enthusiasm, expressed in 1974, did not diminish as the years and productions progressed. If anything, he would have liked to concentrate even more of the staging on the platform itself, reducing or eliminating some of the supplementary scenographic elements and reinforcing others.

The reviews of the production were mixed, enthusiasm alternating with irritation. Not unexpectedly, criteria were often confused or not even stated. Occasionally a wit would dismiss the platform as a "square flying saucer" or the folio strips in *Siegfried* as "fettucine."[9] On the other hand, some critics viewed Svoboda's work as a component of a total production and in relation to a tradition having its source in the visions of Appia and Craig. Tom Sutcliffe, of the *Classical Music Weekly*, wrote:

Josef Svoboda's designs, wholly integrated with Friedrich's conceptions in their practicality, provide some of the most stunning images I have ever seen in the theater. At last Gordon Craig's dreams of the visual impact of which a Wagner production should be capable are being matched. Yet each image, whether it follows or ignores Wagner's wishes, serves to underline clearly aspects of the total work: nothing is there for prettiness or convenience.[10]

Although a similar statement might not be made about the Geneva *Ring* because its total production strategy was not as conducive to the creation of "stunning images" of a Craigian type, Svoboda's scenography at Geneva was significant in revealing the application of a distinctly modern sensibility to more traditional and familiar theatrical forms and methods.

THE GENEVA PRODUCTION

The Geneva *Ring* began its performances four months after the beginning of the Covent Garden cycle and was in large measure produced concurrently with it.[11] Although they were outweighed by contrasts, several similarities between the two versions should be mentioned. In both productions the organization of space developed from the layouts of the two stages, each of which had a very large trap area, which allowed for the single platform at Covent Garden and for the elaborate, multiple platforming at Geneva. Svoboda pointed out that the Geneva scenography was based on an alternative Covent Garden plan that was finally not feasible at Covent Garden. "I sought an alternative plan not involving a platform, and emphasizing the actors—a space that could even be illusional if necessary. Then I proceeded to develop it further." It might even be said that the platform principle did not completely disappear, for it is almost as if the single platform at Covent Garden were fragmented and reorganized into the many small platforms at Geneva; but it must also be noted that the Geneva platforms were never mobile in the course of the action.

Laser projections were a major element in both productions. The laser device and the kind of images projected were the same in both cases, but in Geneva the laser projections were *live*, whereas in Covent Garden they were on film. This meant that the Geneva laser projections were noticeably more vivid but were less precisely and thoroughly planned than the carefully "scored" Covent Garden laser projections. At Geneva the laser projections appeared less tightly related to the dramatic action and more limited to providing atmospheric decor. There was simply not enough time to work out the necessarily complex scoring, and the overall effect was somewhat more impressionistic and vague.

Other points of similarity may be perceived, but fundamentally Svoboda's treatment was different. Similarly, the ideas of the two directors showed fundamental differences. Like Götz Friedrich, Jean-Claude Riber eschewed an interpretation along historical, much less naturalistic lines and resolutely opposed any narrow ideological or socially relevant message. But while both saw the *Ring* as a parable not only of nineteenth-century bourgeois society but also of universal, eternal forces, Friedrich adopted a more detached, critical view of society's evolution, and Riber a more emotive interpretation stressing interior, archetypal processes. In staging, while Friedrich exploited the world-as-stage and stage-as-world metaphor, Riber sought a flexible ambience that would encompass the divergent elements of the four operas in a more general aesthetic unity. Riber's final remarks in program notes for the total *Ring* are characteristic:

[Wagner] wants to create associations of ideas, but at the same time a world, the aspects of which do not form the frame of a historically precise situation, or correspond to . . . programs or ideologies. He wants a world whose conditions go beyond human possibilities . . . a world in the image of the universe. . . .The understanding proposed by Wagner does not exclude the existence of the enigmatic. In this sense, what is important for me is not a realistic, historically accurate mise-en-scène but one based on emotional and visual fantasy.[12]

On the one hand, Riber accentuated the humanity of the characters and their personal, familial relationships rather than their abstract identity as embodiments of this or that principle. Riber's direction also emphasized the increasingly anthropomorphic element in the sequence of operas as the power of the gods decreases in the face of human forces. This shift was brought out by

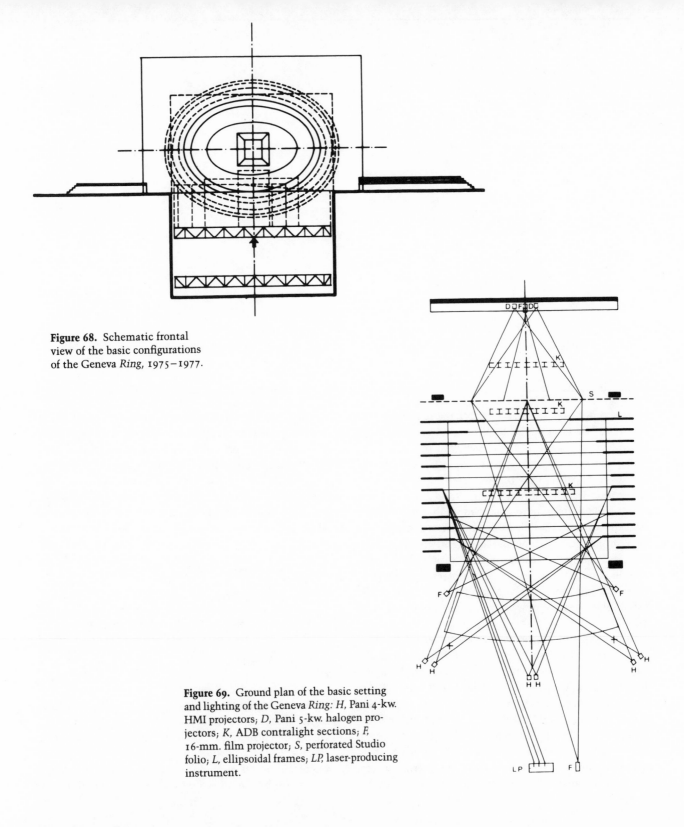

Figure 68. Schematic frontal
view of the basic configurations
of the Geneva *Ring*, 1975–1977.

Figure 69. Ground plan of the basic setting
and lighting of the Geneva *Ring: H,* Pani 4-kw.
HMI projectors; *D,* Pani 5-kw. halogen projectors; *K,* ADB contralight sections; *F,*
16-mm. film projector; *S,* perforated Studio
folio; *L,* ellipsoidal frames; *LP,* laser-producing
instrument.

the more human, personalized quality of the acting; by the costuming (for example, Brünnhilde only briefly wore armor; for most of her appearances she wore a soft, draped smock); and by the generally low-key, Rembrandt-like lighting (generally dark with occasional highlights), which was reminiscent of the Bayreuth *Tristan*, as well as the projections of mountains, clouds, and forests, which added an almost naturalistic dimension. In contrast, Riber presented much of the action abstractly, even statically, like an oratorio. An outstanding example was the blocking for the ride of the Valkyries, which was extremely formal, controlled, almost static. The resulting staging lacked the dramatic confrontations and interactions of the cycle at Covent Garden but possessed a productive inner tension between opposing tendencies: the emotional (even romantic) and the austere; the traditional and the modern; the concrete and the abstract; the realistic and the distinctly stylized.

The scenographer's task was less a matter of seeking an appropriate "instrument" and more a matter of seeking a metaphorically expressive "design" in the traditional sense. What resulted, as the illustrations reveal, was the central image of an ellipse, more precisely a series of parallel elliptical forms suggesting a nucleus, a

womb, or a cell, which had both human and technological associations. (Certainly it would appear to have been the basis of the subsequent ellipsoid in the Geneva *Tristan*, which Riber also directed.) (plate 13, figs. 68, 69.)

The ambivalence or inner tension of varied connotations perceivable in Riber's staging of the human drama was also present in Svoboda's scenography, which sustained a tension between traditional and modern forms. The ellipses were essentially a variation of the traditional wing-and-drop form but with a distinctly modern, architectonic quality. Similarly, although this wing-and-drop system was treated very pictorially and with colors, the colors were entirely created by lighting, for the ellipses themselves were a neutral gray; the effect was that of scene painting with light. One of Svoboda's observations is relevant to this matter: "Scenery by means of lighting rather than paint is the future, because the individual artist can do exactly what he wants and then have it projected, thereby really conveying the artist's signature and possessing quality."

Moreover, by using projections of photographs (particularly black and white or monochromatic photographs), Svoboda gave distance and a modern look to otherwise representational, natural images of mountains, forests,

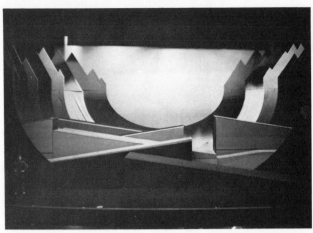

Figure 70. Geneva *Walküre*, 1976, set under worklights, showing the semielliptical forms with added jagged tops and angled platform units to convey the effect of violated unity as well as a mountainous area. *Photograph by Jarka Burian.*

Figure 71. The opening scene of the Geneva *Rheingold*, 1975, showing the Rhine maidens reflected by the horizontal mirrored bands suspended above the stage.

and clouds. A similar artistic tension existed between the potentially romantic background images and the purely architectonic, formal elements of the bare wooden platforms constituting the acting areas between the parallel ellipses. These alternatively level or angled ramps created an aesthetic counterforce to the traditional nineteenth-century associations of the scenography. Needless to say, the laser projections added to this underlying aesthetic tension.

In a larger sense, the scenography also embodied the disruption of an established order that the operas depict: the stealing of the gold, the rape of the ring itself, and the subsequent acts of violence and treachery. The ellipse as a coherent, complete form was evident only in *Das Rheingold*; in each of the subsequent operas it was fractured, incomplete. In *Die Walküre*, for example, one saw only the lower halves of the ellipses; the top of each had a jagged, broken profile, as if the very core of nature had been cracked open (fig. 70). In *Siegfried*, the ellipses still retained only their bottom halves; extending above them were jagged vertical forms, thus maintaining the sense of disharmony and fragmentation. *Götterdämmerung* conveyed a sense of artificial healing, a deceptive appearance of order in that the bottom halves of the

ellipses had smooth tops, but one realized that the ellipses were still essentially but a fragment of their former selves.

Das Rheingold

In Geneva, as in London's Covent Garden, *Das Rheingold* began with the expansion of a laser projection from a single small point to swirling, spreading patterns, which also indicated still another difference: the basic design and stage layout in Geneva allowed the projections to cover a larger area, which was one reason why Svoboda had projections play a greater role in this *Ring* than at Covent Garden. The opening scene presented another echo of Covent Garden: the Rhine maidens and Alberich were reflected in three horizontal mirrored bands hung above the green-lighted stage like venetian blinds, thereby reinforcing the impression of the figures being in a watery world (fig. 71).

One of the most striking projected "painted" effects in *Das Rheingold* was the rainbow spectrum leading to Valhalla. Here the ellipses themselves formed the spectrum as a result of having the rear of each elliptical frame lined with colored lights that illuminated the front of the elliptical frame behind it. Before the revival

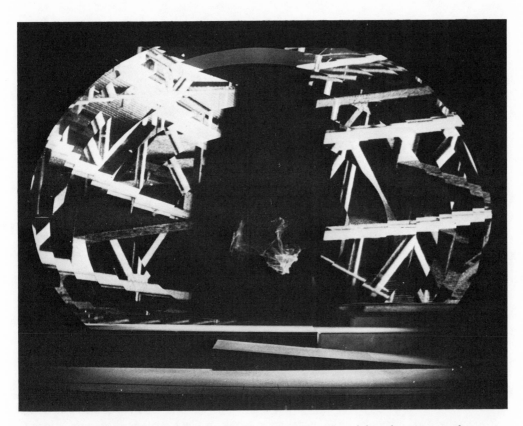

Figure 72. The Nibelheim scene in the Geneva *Rheingold*. The effect of the subterranean realm was created by a full stage projection of vast timbers, like those found in a mine. Note the laser projection in the center. Compare with figure 49.

Figure 77. The inflated and suspended dragon of *Siegfried*, act 2, is seen in relation to the jagged tops of the lower half of the ellipses and the jagged suspended panels supplementing them.

tion but more selective and built of heterogeneous, modern elements (plate 15). The subsequent forest scenes were depicted by fullstage projections of dense, dark foliage onto the ellipses and a series of vertical, jagged-edged elements suspended above the stage (fig. 76). The Geneva stage had an essentially empty central space for these scenes, unlike the Covent Garden stage with its relatively thick clusters of strips, but the feeling of density was present in Geneva as a result of the lighting and projections.

Two other scenographic moments in the Geneva *Siegfried* warrant mentioning. The Geneva dragon was an inflated object lowered from the flies, thus leading to the especially vivid effect of its deflated collapse once Siegfried stabbed it (fig. 77).[13] In *Rheingold*, Erda was abstracted to a beam of light, but in *Siegfried*, in keeping with the greater degree of the human element, she appeared physically downstage left, raised and lowered on a small lift from below stage (fig. 78).

Götterdämmerung

Götterdämmerung followed most of the special tendencies already noted with regard to the lighting, the acting, and the projections. New motifs or elements included the basic metaphor or image chosen to dominate the world of this opera: a frozen, crystallized society, conveyed by projections of frost and ice, and a general absence of color in the Gibichung scenes (plate 16). Even the outdoor scenes, for example the hunting party, were presented in a more abstract and muted manner than in *Siegfried*.

A notable new element in *Götterdämmerung* was a very large square frame suspended at various heights above the stage. In a way, it might be considered the equivalent of the many glass panels in the Covent Garden production, but that is perhaps a forced comparison. In any case it not only was an interesting element of pure design (in relation to the elliptical curves) but reinforced the connotations of hardness and coldness in the rest of the setting (plate 17). Specifically, the rear of the frame was covered by a transparent glass folio that added a glistening quality. Originally, the rear was to have been covered by a perforated mirror folio in order to reflect the actual audience at certain moments, perhaps to press the analogy between the world of the Gibichungs and present society. The mirror folio was not used because the panels of folio could not be welded without the seams showing. The glass folio could be

Figure 78. The encounter of Wotan and Erda in the Geneva *Siegfried*, act 3, scene 1, is another example of how the projections obliterated the elliptical forms in the middle two operas.

invisibly welded, however, and so presented an unbroken surface. The front of the frame was covered by scrim, which occasionally took abstract, textured projections from the sides, projections of crystalline forms or of highly textured glass.

During Siegfried's funeral music the frame functioned almost exactly the way the glass panels did at Covent Garden (figs. 79, 80). It was lowered to mask Siegfried's body completely as the general lights were brought very low; then a glow seemed to emanate from Siegfried's body behind the scrim, creating another characteristically Rembrandt-like lighting effect in this production. As an exception to the general pattern, the funeral music played with an open curtain, and the transition to the Gibichung Hall was made as it was at Covent Garden: when the lights came up we saw through the scrim a tableau of soldiers around Siegfried's body, and as the scrim lifted, other characters entered to make it evident that the action had shifted from the forest to the hall.

The culminating moments of *Götterdämmerung* at Geneva were broadly comparable to those at Covent Garden except for the absence of the tilting platform and the special fiery funeral-pyre device. Instead, at Geneva, laser projections conveyed more of the sense of the final conflagration and collapse, supplemented by straight projections of fire on the entire set. At the very end, the Valhalla cube reappeared, but covered with projected flames. Then the upper half of the ellipses (which had not been present since *Das Rheingold*) slowly lowered to within about a yard of the lower half, an ambivalent conclusion. On the one hand, the cycle was not complete; the integrity of the ellipses was not final. On the other hand, the green flow of laser rays conveyed a sense of the restored purity of the Rhine, and finally only the original red laser dot remained against a vague blue laser background. We had returned to the initial visual image of *Das Rheingold*, all but the unbroken unity of the ellipses.

The impression left by the Geneva *Ring* was that of a more pictorial, more color-loaded, more traditionally "designed" production than that at Covent Garden. Geneva represented a fusion of a number of Svoboda's scenographic techniques, chiefly an architectonic organization of stage space and a varied use of projections,

Figure 79. The slain Siegfried in 1977 *Götterdämmerung*, act 3, scene 1, at Geneva: a very austere scenographic treatment of the hunting scene, limited to projections of snow and frost. Compare with the Covent Garden version, figure 64. *Photograph by Jarka Burian.*

Figure 80. The body of Siegfried in the Gibichung Hall, act 3, scene 2; transition from forest to hall was accomplished by lowering of framed scrim to the floor, thus masking Siegfried during the scene change. *Photograph by Jarka Burian.*

with an older tradition of painted scenery. His tendency toward abstract, metaphoric images applied to both. Dramatically, as a total production, it recounted an action rather than taking a critical, questioning stance toward it; its tone was realistic, emotive, personal rather than detached or ironic. Taken together, the two productions demonstrated two types of modern interpretation, two types of modern mise-en-scènes of Wagner that clearly embodied a post-neo-Bayreuth sensibility. At the same time, they did not sacrifice essential Wagnerian elements to a narrow, explicit allegorical "statement" or to a radical disassembling and restructuring of the Wagnerian motifs of action and scene.

Chapter 7 *Die Meistersinger*

Not only does the 1978 Prague production of *Die Meistersinger* represent Svoboda's most recent work on a Wagner opera,[1] but *Die Meistersinger* is also among Wagner's most mature operas (coming between *Tristan* and *Siegfried*) as well as his sole comic opera. It has been called Wagner's aesthetic and ethical testament to humanity, a genial treatment of love, the conflict of old and new traditions in art and society, and a celebration of a people's cultural unity. The opera itself involves a creative contrast between the historical subject matter of the German Renaissance and Wagner's distinctive nineteenth-century musical composition. It is this contrast or tension (somewhat similar to that noted in the Geneva *Ring*) that formed the basis of this production.

As the director Václav Kašlík observed in the program notes, the production was not concerned with the historicism and genre naturalism that usually mark stagings of this opera. Even the costumes were designed to blend elements of early sixteenth-century Germany with the style of Wagner's day. Similarly, Svoboda's scenery combines the historical period of the opera with a modern treatment: on the one hand, the wooden material and construction of the period embodied in a trip-

tych formed by Gothic arches or in a wooden rosette; on the other hand, a consciously created, modern artistic reality in the clean-cut simplicity and stylization of the design (fig. 81). Moreover, as Kašlík pointed out, "Svoboda's setting accentuates still another characteristic of this opera—its strong stageworthiness and theatricality; that is, not a naturalistic picture of old Nuremberg, but a strongly, theatrically stylized, unifying basis for the whole opera in the form of a triptych solely of wood." Kašlík went on to refer to the tension created between the many realistic aspects of the opera and the stylization inherent in the staging as "the counterpoint that supports most operas. We express the stylization of the music by stylized settings, and the truthfulness of the character relationships by realistic performance."

Svoboda's scenography here seems aimed at providing a visually strong but austere environment within which the music and the interplay of characters can find their fullest expression with least distraction. The specific elements of the set are completely appropriate to Wagner's action but clearly the product of a contemporary sensibility. Once again Svoboda provides a versatile unit setting, which consists of the triptych of wooden beams

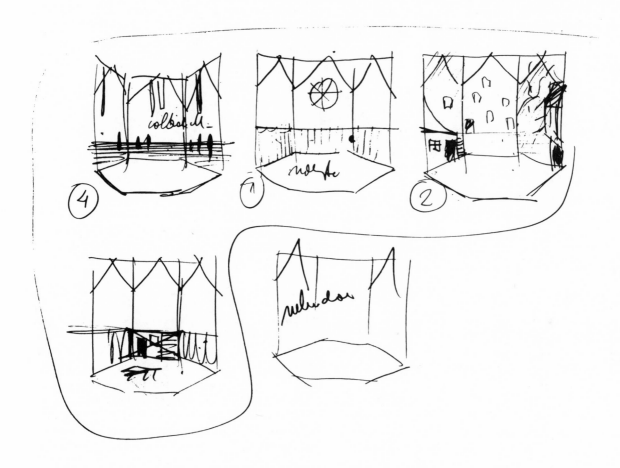

Figure 81. Svoboda's sketch indicates the variations in the basic setting of *Die Meistersinger*. The Gothic design motif of the pointed arch is maintained throughout.

Figure 82. Act 1 of *Die Meistersinger*, Prague, 1978. Although stage directions indicate the interior of a church, Svoboda includes buildings as well. *Photograph by Jaromír Svoboda.*

Figure 83. *Die Meistersinger*, act 3, scene 1. Sachs's workshop is created within the context of the basic setting by closing the permanent scrim drapes and adding a wooden wall. The wooden stairs visible through the door are ready for the crowd scene that follows. *Photograph by Jaromír Svoboda.*

in the Gothic style and units of steps that have a number of uses. To these elements are added a few others to create the four scenes of the opera: wooden Gothic facades, wooden pews and a large wooden rosette, unobtrusive scrim drapes, and essential props and furniture, many items of which are subtly anachronistic in developing the tension between the time of the original story and the time of Wagner's composition. The omnipresent method of modulated, expressive lighting provides accent, spatial dimension, atmosphere, and vitality to all the rest (figs. 82, 83).

It is essentially a simpler scenography than is evident in his other Wagner productions, closer to its sources in everyday reality, in keeping with this most realistic of Wagner's operas. It demonstrates clearly that Svoboda is not bound to sophisticated techniques of projections, mirrors, kinetics, and electronics but that he can create with understated eloquence and adapt his multiple talents to the inherent values of the work itself and its particular production concept. Equally evident are some of the characteristics that underlie even his most complex, sophisticated work: an architect's sense of space and strong architectonic design; a theatrically cultivated

awareness of the need of a set to be functional rather than decorative, a preference for abstract simplicity rather than luxuriant embellishment.

It is scenography that is deceptively simple and plain, for it bears the hallmarks of mature, balanced artistry, a sense of design wedded to function, an almost classical restraint that provides a maximum of expressiveness with a minimum of overt effort. It provides additional evidence that Svoboda's work represents neither an effort at radical reinterpretations of texts nor a private, surrealist vision but a constant search and striving for more fully expressive means, for ideally viable, functional, theatrically oriented instruments or principles with which to realize most fully the visions of playwrights, directors, or universal geniuses like Wagner.

PART THREE CONCLUSION AND POSTSCRIPT

Figure 84. Joseph Svoboda standing in the Teatro Olympico, Vicenza, early 1970's.

Conclusion

In retrospect, Svoboda's scenography for Wagner is impressive in the sheer range of its forms and techniques, as well as in Svoboda's ability to evolve creative variations of many of them. This ability is rooted in Svoboda's alert responsiveness to the stimuli of music, libretto, directorial concept, and even the structural characteristic of a given theater building. But it also springs from his finding inspiration in the very medium with which he works: "As the Renaissance sculptor knew his medium of stone or metal, the scenographer must know his contemporary techniques, materials, and technical devices. Only then may a wonderful thing happen: these expressive materials and techniques may become a source of inspiration to us."

Allowing for its characteristic hyperbole, Edward Gordon Craig's prophecy in 1905 seems singularly prescient with regard to Svoboda:

I look for a Renaissance of the theatre . . . through the advent of a man who shall contain in him all the qualities that go to make up a master of the theatre, and through the reform of the theatre as an instrument. When that is accomplished, when the theatre has become a masterpiece of mechanism, when it has invented a technique, it will without any effort develop a creative art of its own.[1]

The many examples of Svoboda's scenography for Wagner demonstrate, I believe, that Svoboda is indeed in the line of theater workers whose primary dedication is not to dramatic literature, music, or visual art but to the evolution of the art of the theater. Symptomatic of his approach is Svoboda's frequent observation that "the ideal is a scenography that will not borrow expressive means from other disciplines of visual art but will evolve its own creative alphabet." Moreover, at its best, and with remarkable consistency, Svoboda's scenography *bridges* what Craig cites as two phases of theater's evolution; that is, theater as "a masterpiece of mechanism" and theater as a "creative art."

There are those who are alarmed if not offended by Craig's image of theater as mechanism, as there are those who feel uneasy with the technical elements of Svoboda's scenography, who assume that art and technology are incompatible or fear that Svoboda's scenography becomes an end in itself. Usually underlying such attitudes is the premise that the text and the actor are the essence of theater and that a relatively bare platform would probably serve them adequately. A more judicious view is that theater at its fullest and richest requires not only actor, script, costume, and choreography but also expressive scenography, whether it consists of nothing more than sensitively modulated lighting or the full range of effects evident in productions like Svoboda's *Tannhäuser* or *Ring*. Moreover, scenography itself may become an "actor," as it often does in Svoboda's work, communicating the essence of a playwright's or director's vision perhaps more tellingly at times than performer or text.

Like any other artist, Svoboda is compelled to express his special talent and craft. There have undoubtedly been times when his scenography has dominated a production. Such occasions, however, are less likely to have been the result of Svoboda's will to power than of a breakdown of communication, an imbalance of talents, or several external circumstances. Svoboda is too practical a man of theater, as well as inherently too tactful, to insist on imposing his special strengths on a production to the detriment of the production as a whole. He has clearly stated his own attitude:

Scenography does not evolve on its own but only in a tight alliance with other elements of a play on stage, because without them it cannot exist.

[Our] expressive means—new or old—should remain non-intrusive, never ends in themselves, but serve the production as a whole. They should be used only when dramatically necessary; otherwise we discredit both them and ourselves.

In 1974, when the two *Rings* were starting to be produced, Svoboda spoke of his ongoing efforts and the excitement they generated within him. His remarks captured the complexity of his work and vision and also put into proper perspective his means and ends:

I dream of a light on stage which by means of an interference of light waves will be precisely where I want it to be and its source not visible. That is, its rays will not be visible; they're a problem because they create special design effects that are not always wanted. Whoever gets things like this in hand will be a great poet and do fantastic things. That's what I envy in those rascals to come—new techniques such as I have experienced with lighting and projections. But banality and "effects" must be avoided. One must think in terms of theater, a place where poetry can be created.

Postscript

Nearly four years will have elapsed between the time the main body of this book was written and its publication. The disadvantage of this is that the reader learns not what Svoboda has been doing recently, but what he was doing at least five years ago. In an effort to bring the text factually up to date, Appendix B lists his work in theater from the 1971–72 season through the 1981–82 season. (His earlier work is listed in *The Scenography of Josef Svoboda.*) But more important is to note the nature and direction of what he has been doing since the last of his Wagner productions, *Die Meistersinger*, in 1978. In that regard, the passage of time has been an advantage in that it provides a valuable perspective. Not only does it allow us to note his current tendencies but, more significantly, it allows for a more detached estimation of Svoboda's scenographic achievement in the Wagner productions.

Looking back, I believe one sees more clearly that productions such as the London *Tannhäuser*, both *Rings*, and the last two *Tristans* probably meant a high watermark of Svoboda's richly expressive use of highly sophisticated technical instruments and materials. Budgets and staffs were ample, and Svoboda exploited his opportunities. Since then, the international economy has made it unlikely that comparable opportunities will arise again soon, even if Svoboda were inclined to seek still more advanced and elaborate "masterpieces of mechanism." But the point is that Svoboda has not been so inclined. Although he has not renounced modern technology's potential contribution to heightened, richer scenographic expressiveness, he has felt the need to step back and take a breath, to reexamine what he has been doing. In retrospect, indeed, the *Meistersinger* production of 1978 may be considered both symptomatic and prophetic.

More specifically, when I saw Svoboda in April 1982, he was involved with final rehearsals of a production of *Hamlet* in Prague's Smetana Theatre. I attended the last dress rehearsal. The scenography would have been considered austere even by the criteria of a Jacques Copeau; for Svoboda it was as if a gourmet had deliberately chosen to fast on bread and water. The stage was empty of everything save black drapes, several shallow steps running the width of the stage, and the minimum of furniture. No projections, kinetics, or other marvels. Lighting, yes—but neither atmospheric nor virtuosic.

Instead, the lighting remained at a relatively high intensity on the stage as a whole, "so as not to allow the actors to hide," as Svoboda put it.

I questioned Svoboda as to what lay behind this exceptionally restrained, spare turn his work had taken. His answer had nothing pat about it. It revealed the effort of an artist to put into words a fundamental shift (temporary or not, who can say?) in his feeling and thinking about his work. It seems to me appropriate to conclude this study with an extract of his remarks on that occasion, for they represent if not an antithesis then at least an alternative to the words of his which ended the main text of this book a page or two ago. The two sets of remarks indicate, I believe, a necessary dialectic in his creative process, not overtly constant but never entirely absent.

In attempting to define the essence of this—for him —different scenography, he used the term "divadlo nula," zero theater:

It means theater returning to its own essence rather than relying on other media. Not rejecting other media or means but making more precise just *how* to use them . . . while starting from the beginning again, from fundamental principles. In this *Hamlet* and other [recent] productions I've tried to create space by minimal expressive means, using the basic space of the stage and reworking it for a given play with a minimum of elements, and with more emphasis on the actor. . . . Not weighing down the space, but discovering again just what "information" is *necessary* at given moments. . . . This "ascetism" in creating space attracts me now, by means of lighting for example . . . psychological space, without the usual Svoboda signatures. I'd like to test this systematically —restricting myself to *functional* needs, forcing myself to find the *best* means or method. . . . It will lead, ultimately, to a discovery of new paths. The "zero scene" is a starting point for a reexamination of [my] accumulated principles and "systems": curtains, flats, stairs, mirrors, projections, and so on. . . . It's the only way to rid myself of what's already done, even "forget" what's happened. I rarely see the work of others or read books on scenography . . . I don't even want to know what *I've* done. (I tell students to ignore my work.) . . . It's a way of forcing myself to think like a director and not simply *deliver* scenography on order. . . . It's a matter of instinct. I *could* develop my usual approach and methods further but I no longer *like* it. I want to be simpler . . . purer.

Appendix A: The Covent Garden Platform

Since the kinetic, transformable platform is the central expressive component of the Covent Garden *Ring* and is highly regarded by Svoboda as an ideal metaphoric and functional scenographic instrument, its specifications warrant itemization.

Platform

Dimensions   37' × 32' × 2'
Weight   3.5 tons
Weight of step units and drives *(Rheingold)*   2.25 tons

Tower assembly

Overall length, closed   13'6"
Maximum extension, two sections   12'2"

Elevation

Maximum speed of lifting-rams operation (infinitely variable)   10 ft./min.
Thrust per ram, maximum   5 tons

Rotation

Maximum rotational speed of platform   1 rpm

Inclination

Maximum single angle, all four planes   45°
Maximum diagonal compound angle   35°
Maximum time from level to 45°   20 secs.

Appendix B: Svoboda Productions, 1971-1982

The following list brings up to date a similar list in *The Scenography of Josef Svoboda*. Titles of works other than German, French, or Italian are in English.

Author and Title	Place of Performance	Date of Premiere	Director
P. I. Tchaikovsky *Eugene Onegin*	Municipal Theater Frankfurt/Main, GFR	November 1971	V. Kašlík
G. Verdi *Simone Boccanegra*	National Theater Prague	December 1971	V. Kašlík
W. Gombrowicz *Operetta*	Schiller Theater Berlin, GFR	January 1972	E. Schröder
L. Janáček *From the House of the Dead*	State Opera Hamburg, GFR	January 1972	J. Dexter
A. Chekhov *The Sea Gull*	Theater behind the Gate Prague	March 1972	O. Krejča
R. B. Sheridan *The School for Scandal*	National Theater Prague	March 1972	M. Macháček
G. Verdi *Nabucco*	Covent Garden London	March 1972	V. Kašlík
R. Strauss *Don Juan*	National Theater Prague	May 1972	J. Nemeček
R. Strauss *Tyl Eulenspiegel*	National Theater Prague	May 1972	V. Jílek
I. Stravinsky *Le sacre du printemps*	National Theater Prague	May 1972	E. Gabzdyl

Author and Title	Place of Performance	Date of Premiere	Director
I. Stravinsky *The Rake's Progress*	National Theater Prague	June 1972	K. Jernek
G. Bizet *Carmen*	Metropolitan Opera New York	September 1972	G. Gentele
M. P. Musorgski *Boris Godunov*	State Opera Hamburg, GFR	September 1972	J. Dexter
P. Zindel *The Effect of Gamma Rays on Man-in-the-Moon Marigolds*	National Theater Prague	October 1972	J. Pleskot
A. N. Scriabin *Poem of Fire*	La Scala Milan	October 1972	V. Peucher
I. Stravinsky *L'oiseau de feu*	Royal Theater Copenhagen	November 1972	E. Holm
B. Brecht *Die Dreigroschenoper*	Municipal Theater Zurich	December 1972	H. Buckwitz
E. Suchon *The Whirlpool*	National Theater Prague	January 1973	P. Kočí
L. Janáček *Kata Kabanová*	Opera House Zurich	April 1973	H. Buckwitz
B. Smetana *The Secret*	National Theater Prague	May 1973	P. Kočí
T. Stoppard *The Jumpers*	Burgtheater Vienna	May 1973	P. Wood
M. Gorki *Children of the Sun*	National Theater Prague	June 1973	J. Kačer

Author and Title	Place of Performance	Date of Premiere	Director
R. Wagner *Tannhäuser*	Covent Garden London	September 1973	V. Kašlík
I. Dvorecky *The Man from Elsewhere*	National Theater Prague	November 1973	M. Macháček
P. I. Tchaikovsky *Sleeping Beauty*	National Theater Prague	December 1973	P. Weigel
A. B. Valecho *A Dream of Reason*	Moscow Art Theater Moscow	December 1973	O. N. Jefremov
G. Verdi *I vespri siciliani*	Metropolitan Opera New York	January 1974	J. Dexter
T. Stoppard *The Jumpers*	Kennedy Center Washington, D.C.	February 1974	P. Wood
J. Racine *Phèdre*	Slovene National Theater Ljubljana	February 1974	H. I. Pilikian
J. Cikker *Coriolanus*	National Theater Prague	April 1974	P. Kočí
G. Verdi *Don Carlos*	Municipal Theater Cologne, GFR	April 1974	H. Neugebauer
Prague Carnival	Laterna Magika Prague	April 1974	V. Kašlík
I. Bukovcan *Snow on the Limba*	National Theater Prague	May 1974	V. Hudeček
B. Smetana *The Devil's Wall*	National Theater Prague	May 1974	V. Kašlík

Author and Title	Place of Performance	Date of Premiere	Director
R. Wagner *Tristan und Isolde*	Festival Theater Bayreuth, GFR	July 1974	A. Everding
E. Rostand *Cyrano de Bergerac*	Festival Theater Prague	September 1974	M. Macháček
H. Berlioz *Les Troyens*	Grand Theater Geneva	September 1974	J.-C. Riber
R. Wagner *Das Rheingold*	Covent Garden London	September 1974	G. Friedrich
R. Wagner *Die Walküre*	Covent Garden London	October 1974	G. Friedrich
V. Vishnevsky *An Optimistic Tragedy*	National Theater Prague	January 1975	M. Macháček
R. Wagner *Das Rheingold*	Grand Theater Geneva	January 1975	J.-C. Riber
J. Radickov *The Snow Laughed as It Fell*	National Theater Studio Prague	February 1975	L. Vymětal
H. Berlioz *Symphonie fantastique*	National Opera Paris	March 1975	R. Petit
F. Schiller *Kabale und Liebe*	Akademie Theater Vienna	March 1975	G. Klingenberg
L. Tolstoi *War and Peace*	National Theater Prague	April 1975	P. Ansimov
Love in Carnival Colors	Laterna Magika Prague	April 1975	V. Kašlík E. Schorm

Author and Title	Place of Performance	Date of Premiere	Director
P. Weigel *Bartolucci*	Théâtre Espace Pierre Cardin Paris	June 1975	P. Weigel
L. Beethoven *Fidelio*	Opera House Zurich	September 1975	C. H. Drese
L. Janáček *Jenufa*	National Theater Prague	September 1975	P. Kočí
R. Wagner **Siegfried**	Covent Garden London	September 1975	G. Friedrich
P. Folta *The Lost Fairy Tale*	Laterna Magika Prague	October 1975	J. Jireš
B. Brecht *Mahagonny*	Grand Theater Geneva	October 1975	J.-C. Riber
G. Verdi *Simone Boccanegra*	Opera House Zurich	October 1975	V. Kašlík
F. Grillparzer *König Otakar*	Burgtheater Vienna	January 1976	G. Klingenberg
R. Wagner **Die Walküre**	Grand Theater Geneva	January 1976	J.-C. Riber
G. Bizet *Passion*	National Theater Prague	January 1976	P. Weigel
G. Puccini *Turandot*	Teatro Reggio Turin	March 1976	J.-C. Riber
L. Beethoven *Fidelio*	National Theater Prague	April 1976	P. Kočí

Author and Title	Place of Performance	Date of Premiere	Director
R. Wagner *Siegfried*	Grand Theater Geneva	June 1976	J.-C. Riber
G. Verdi *Otello*	National Opera Paris	June 1976	T. Hands
P. I. Tchaikovsky *Queen of Spades*	National Arts Centre Ottawa	July 1976	V. Kašlík
R. Wagner *Götterdämmerung*	Covent Garden London	September 1976	G. Friedrich
W. Shakespeare *The Tempest*	Berlin Tournament Munich	September 1976	E. Schroder
J. Vrchlický *The Trial of Love*	National Theater Prague	October 1976	J. Pleskot
B. A. Zimmermann *Die Soldaten*	State Opera Hamburg	November 1976	G. Friedrich
G. Verdi *Don Carlos*	Grand Theater Geneva	January 1977	J.-C. Riber
The Magic Circus	Laterna Magika Prague	April 1977	E. Schorm
M. Stieber *The Last Vacation*	National Theater Prague	May 1977	M. Macháček
C. Gounod *Faust*	State Opera Berlin, GDR	May 1977	V. Kašlík
R. Wagner *Götterdämmerung*	Grand Theater Geneva	May 1977	J.-C. Riber

Author and Title	Place of Performance	Date of Premiere	Director
R. Strauss *Ariadne auf Naxos*	National Arts Centre Ottawa	July 1977	V. Kašlík
F. Dürrenmatt *Ein Engel kommt nach Babylon*	Opera House Zurich	July 1977	G. Friedrich
J. Gellman *Closed Circuit*	Moscow Art Theater Moscow	October 1977	O. N. Jefremov
B. Vasiljev *White Storks above Brest*	National Theater Prague	October 1977	V. Hudeček
R. Strauss *Die Frau ohne Schatten*	Grand Theater Geneva	January 1978	J.-C. Riber
G. Verdi *Macbeth*	National Theater Prague	January 1978	V. Kašlík
G. Verdi *Il Trovatore*	Opera House Zurich	February 1978	F. Enriquez
C. Goldoni *Il Campiello*	National Theater Prague	March 1978	M Macháček
L. Janáček *Jenufa*	Juilliard School New York	April 1978	G. Freedman
G. Verdi *Nabucco*	Grand Theater Geneva	April 1978	G. Klingenberg
R. Wagner **Tristan und Isolde**	Grand Theater Geneva	September 1978	J.-C. Riber
B. Smetana *The Bartered Bride*	Metropolitan Opera New York	October 1978	J. Dexter

Author and Title	Place of Performance	Date of Premiere	Director
R. Wagner *Die Meistersinger*	National Theater Prague	November 1978	V. Kašlík
L. Janáček *From the House of the Dead*	Opera House Zurich	November 1978	G. Friedrich
L. Beethoven *Fidelio*	Grand Theater Geneva	December 1978	C. H. Drese
G. Verdi *La Traviata*	National Theater Prague	January 1979	P. Weigel
L. Janáček *The Makropulos Affair*	State Theater Hannover	January 1979	V. Kašlík
L. Stroupežnický *Our Militants*	National Theater Prague	March 1979	M. Macháček
H. C. Andersen *The Snow Queen*	Laterna Magika Prague	May 1979	E. Schorm P. Šmok
J. Hašek *The Good Soldier Schweik*	Schiller Theater Berlin, GFR	June 1979	H. Buckwitz
G. Puccini *Gianni Schicchi* and *Suor Anglica*	National Art Centre Banff, Canada	August 1979	L. Major
R. Petit *Parisiana*	Municipal Theatre Marseille	November 1979	R. Petit
G. Verdi *Don Carlos*	Opera House Zurich	November 1979	J.-C. Riber
K. Čapek *The White Disease*	Tyl Theater Prague	February 1980	M. Macháček

Author and Title	Place of Performance	Date of Premiere	Director
A. Strindberg *The Dream Play*	State University Albany, N.Y.	March 1980	J. Burian
B. Bartok *The Miraculous Mandarin*	La Scala Milan	March 1980	R. Petit
L. Janáček *Jenufa*	Grand Theater Geneva	April 1980	E. Schorm
A. Dvořák *Rusalka*	State Theater Stuttgart	May 1980	E. Schorm
L. Fišer Grief over the Message from Ur	National Theater Prague	May 1980	M. Kůra P. Weigel
I. Zeljenka *The Hero*	National Theater Prague	May 1980	F. Pokorný
V. Kučera *A Flawless Life*	National Theater Prague	May 1980	J. Blážek
G. Verdi *Otello*	Grand Theater Geneva	June 1980	J.-C. Riber
B. McDonald *Time out of Mind*	National Art Centre Banff, Canada	July 1980	B. McDonald
O. Daněk *The Duchess of Wallenstein's Armies*	National Theater Prague	December 1980	M. Macháček
A. Máša *Night Rehearsal*	Laterna Magika Prague	February 1981	E. Schorm
R. Strauss *Josefs Legende*	La Scala Milan	April 1981	F. Flindt

Author and Title	Place of Performance	Date of Premiere	Director
J. W. Goethe *Faust*	National Theater Prague	April 1981	V. Hudeček
W. A. Mozart *Idomeneo*	National Arts Centre Ottawa	July 1981	V. Kašlík
K. Orff *Die Kluge*	Smetana Theater Prague	September 1981	K. Jernek
B. Bartok *Duke Bluebeard's Castle*	Smetana Theater Prague	September 1981	K. Jernek
L. Janáček *From the House of the Dead*	Deutsche Oper Berlin, GFR	October 1981	G. Friedrich
J. Offenbach *The Tales of Hoffmann*	Smetana Theater Prague	October 1981	P. Darrell
Aeschylus *The Oresteia*	Tyl Theater Prague	December 1981	E. Schorm
V. Kašlík *The Road*	Smetana Theater Prague	January 1982	K. Jernek
P. I. Tchaikovsky *Queen of Spades*	Houston Opera Houston	January 1982	V. Kašlík
W. Shakespeare *Hamlet*	National Theater Prague	April 1982	M. Macháček
B. Smetana *Dalibor*	Smetana Theater Prague	May 1982	V. Kašlík

Notes

Chapter 1 Josef Svoboda

1. Unless otherwise indicated, all quotations from Svoboda refer to personal conversations rather than published material. The translation is mine.

2. Jarka Burian, *The Scenography of Josef Svoboda* (Middletown, Conn.: Wesleyan University Press, 1971); "Czechoslovakian Stage Design and Scenography, 1914–1938," *Theatre Design and Technology* 41 (Summer 1975): 14–23, 35; 42 (Fall 1975): 23–32.

3. Francis Fergusson, *The Idea of a Theatre* (Princeton, N.J.: Princeton University Press, 1949), pp. 236–40 passim.

Chapter 2 The Staging of Wagner's Operas

1. Suzanne Langer, "Deceptive Analogies," in *Problems of Art* (New York: Charles Scribner's Sons, 1957), p. 79.

2. Bertolt Brecht, "The Modern Theatre Is Epic Theatre," in *Brecht on Theatre*, ed. John Willett (New York: Hill & Wang, 1964), p. 37.

3. Richard Wagner, quoted in Ernest Newman, *A Study of Wagner* (New York: G. P. Putnam's Sons, 1899), p. 81.

4. Newman, *Study of Wagner*, p. 256.

5. George Bernard Shaw, "Preface to the Fourth Edition," *The Perfect Wagnerite*, 4th ed. (London: Constable & Co., 1923), p. ix.

6. Cosima Wagner, quoted in Geoffrey Skelton, *Wagner at Bayreuth* (New York: George Braziller, 1965), p. 130.

7. Adolphe Appia, *Music and the Art of the Theatre*, trans. Robert Corrigan and Mary Douglas Dirks (Coral Gables, Fla.: University of Miami Press, 1962), pp. 104–30 passim.

8. José Ortéga y Gasset, "In Search of Goethe from Within," in *The Dehumanization of Art and Other Essays on Art, Culture, and Literature* (Princeton, N.J.: Princeton University Press, 1948), p. 174; originally written in 1932.

9. Alois Nagler, "Wagnerian Productions in Postwar Bayreuth," in *The German Theatre Today*, ed. Leroy R. Shaw (Austin, Tex.: University of Texas Press, 1963), p. 22.

10. Wagner, quoted in Skelton, *Wagner at Bayreuth*, p. 41.

11. Wagner, quoted in Nagler, "Wagnerian Productions," p. 22.

12. Skelton, *Wagner at Bayreuth*, p. 174.

13. Walter Panofsky, *Wagner: A Pictorial Biography* (New York: Viking Press, 1963), p. 96.

14. Wagner, quoted in Panofsky, *Wagner*, p. 99.

15. Appia, *Music and the Art of the Theatre*, p. 26.

16. Appia, *La mise en scène du drame wagnérien* (Paris: Leon Challey, 1895); *Die Muzik und die Inscenierung* (Munich: Bruckmann, 1899).

17. Appia, *Music and the Art of the Theatre*, p. 72.

18. Heinz Tietjen, quoted in Skelton, *Wagner at Bayreuth*, p. 154.

19. Emil Preetorius, quoted in Skelton, *Wagner at Bayreuth*, p. 154.

20. Wieland Wagner, quoted in Victor Gollancz, *The "Ring" at Bayreuth* (London: Gollancz, 1966), p. 110.

21. Lee Simonson, "From a Wagnerian Rockpile," *Theatre Arts* 30 (1) (January 1948): 42.

22. Nagler, "Wagnerian Productions," p. 30

Chapter 3 *Der Fliegende Holländer*

1. I saw a dress rehearsal of the production in June 1969.
2. August Everding to Jarka Burian, private correspondence, 5 January 1979.
3. For an illustrated account of these and other earlier Svoboda productions, see Burian, *Scenography of Josef Svoboda*.
4. Svoboda prefers the term *contralight* (that is, the German *Kontralicht*) to *backlight*. More than ordinary backlighting, contralighting is based on the effect of special high-intensity, low-voltage lighting instruments that produce a virtual wall or curtain of light, usually in a plane from high upstage slanting down toward the apron. The instruments, as designed and developed years ago by Svoboda's lighting and optics specialist, Miroslav Pflug, employ mirror optics combined with a special coaxial louver. In Europe, where a 220-volt system is standard, a 250-watt, 24-volt lamp with a pointlike filament is used for each subunit. Nine such lamp units are connected in series and are staggered in two rows to form one bank or section of contralights. The manufacturer is ADB (Adrien de Backer of Belgium). An American version (manufactured by P.G.P. Consultants of Montreal and distributed by Kliegl Brothers under the name Contralight 3015) consists of five lamp units (1,000 watts each, connected in parallel) arranged in a straight line to form one bank or section. This version was first used in Svoboda's *Carmen* at New York's Metropolitan Opera in the fall of 1972, when fifty-six banks or sections used a total of 280 kilowatts.

Chapter 4 *Tannhäuser*

1. The term *folio* refers to a highly pliant, translucent plastic cloth or sheeting that is specially designed to take rear (and sometimes frontal) projection. The rear is shiny, the front (toward the audience) matte. The three main types are "Opera" folio (milky white, designed primarily for frontal projection), "Studio" folio (light gray, equally good for rear and frontal projections), and "Show" folio (anthracite gray, most effective for rear projection). Svoboda helped to develop the Show folio. The European manufacturer is Gerriets of Freiburg, West Germany; the United States distributor is Rosco.
2. One experiment that has not yet been used in production was a pneumatic mirror, based on a mirrored plastic being bonded to a pneumatic backing that would enable the mirror to assume a range of surfaces from convex to concave and thereby effect gross changes in the appearance of whatever the mirrored surface reflected. The mirror was to have been used in a production of Sergei Prokofiev's *Fiery Angel* in Milan in 1970, but the production fell through. In fact, that production was to a great extent conceived as a development of the earlier *Tannhäuser* treatment in that a mirrored surface was to have been tilted over a large circular opening in the stage floor to reflect what was in the trap area below the opening as well as whatever was on a turning ring that rimmed the opening. The application of pneumatics to costumes and props will be mentioned in the account of Wagner's *Ring* in Geneva.
3. For more detail on this and other Svoboda productions after 1971, see Jarka Burian, "A Scenographer's Work: Josef Svoboda's Designs, 1971–1975," *Theatre Design and Technology* 12 (2) (Summer 1976): 10–34.
4. Computerized controls by Strand Electric.
5. For example, see Peter Hayworth in the *Observer*, 23 September 1973, and Philip Hope-Wallace in the *Guardian*, 19 September 1973.

6. David Simmons, *Tribune*, 12 October 1973.

7. Max Loppert, *Financial Times*, 27 September 1973.

Chapter 5 *Tristan und Isolde*

1. Wagner, quoted in Newman, *Study of Wagner*, p. 283.

2. Appia, "The Staging of Tristan and Isolde," in *Music and the Art of the Theatre*, p. 198.

3. I saw a performance in August 1974.

Chapter 6 *Der Ring des Nibelungen*

1. I saw the entire cycle in the fall of 1976 after having seen the first two operas in the fall of 1974.

2. Götz Friedrich, "Die Bühne als Welttheater," in *Theaterarbeit an Wagners "Ring,"* ed. Dietrich Mack (Munich: R. Piper & Co., 1978), p. 104.

3. Götz Friedrich, "Utopia and Reality," trans. Eleanor Lewis. The remarks are found on pp. 39–46 of the souvenir program *Der Ring des Nibelungen* issued by the Royal Opera Covent Garden in September 1976. They also appeared in an earlier program, September 1974, for the opening performances of *Rheingold* and *Walküre*, but were on unnumbered pages.

4. Friedrich, "Die Bühne als Welttheater," p. 106.

5. The platform was designed by Tele-Stage Associates of England to basic specifications indicated by Svoboda. The hydraulic pumps at the heart of the system were constructed by the Hydraulic Division of Vickers Racine. The specific information in the text was derived from "Setting the Stage at the Royal Opera," *Vickers News*, 23 August 1974, p. 3. Fuller specifications are provided in Appendix A.

6. Svoboda first used laser projections in Mozart's *Zauberflöte* in Munich in 1970.

7. Friedrich, "Die Bühne als Welttheater," p. 106.

8. Friedrich, "Die Bühne als Welttheater," p. 110.

9. Frank Granville Barker, *Opera News*, 6 December 1975.

10. Tom Sutcliffe, *Classical Music Weekly*, 25 September 1976.

11. I saw the complete cycle in Geneva in the fall of 1977.

12. Jean-Claude Riber, "Moments émotionells et visuels de la fantasie," in the souvenir program *L'Anneau du Nibelung* issued by Grand Théâtre de Genève in the fall of 1977 for the production of the complete cycle, p. 15. Translation mine.

13. Another instance of pneumatics involved the transformation of Alberich into a serpent in *Das Rheingold*. The actor wore a special inflatable costume that was fitted with an unobtrusive hose attached to a compressed-air instrument, which enabled Alberich to swell up markedly, on cue.

Chapter 7 *Die Meistersinger*

1. I saw the production in June 1979.

Conclusion

1. Edward Gordon Craig, "The Art of the Theatre: The First Dialogue," in *The Art of the Theatre* (London: Heinemann, 1911), p. 176. The essay first appeared in 1905 as a separate booklet.